In Sight of Home

Nessa O'Mahony

salmonpoetry

Published in 2009 by
Salmon Poetry
Cliffs of Moher, County Clare, Ireland
Website: www.salmonpoetry.com
Email: info@salmonpoetry.com

ISBN 978-1-907056-07-9

Cover artwork: *Nautical diary #2* by Paul Cowan from istockphoto.com
Cover design & typesetting: Siobhán Hutson

In Memory of Nellie Ó Cléirigh
(1927-2008)

who encouraged me to listen to women's voices

Acknowledgements

I am grateful to the Board of the National Library of Ireland for the permission to consult original material, on which this verse novel is based, from the Butler Archive, Access Number 4205. I am particularly grateful to Colette O'Flaherty, Assistant Keeper at the National Library, who first drew the archive to my attention and whose impeccable transcription was invaluable to me. Thanks are also due to Paula Meehan, who permitted me to quote from her poem, 'Home'.

I would also like to thank the Board and staff of the Djerassi Resident Artists Program at Woodside, California, where I completed the first draft of the verse novel during a month's residency there in July 2005.

Many thanks, too, to Gay Lynch, both for her advice about things Australian and for her kind loan of two books on the history of Australian cookery. I am greatly indebted to the late Nellie Ó Cléirigh for her generous help with, and advice about, historical sources on emigration to Australia and who alerted me to the existence of the workhouse orphans. Thanks also to Mary-Anne Warner, who provided me with the passenger list for the Lancaster and who suggested other sources of web-based information to me. A huge debt is owed to Professor Carol Rumens and Professor Tony Brown of Bangor University for their astute reading of the various drafts. Thanks too to Patrick Chapman and Joseph O'Connor for their constructive suggestions.

This novel is dedicated to my parents, Donal and Mai O'Mahony, and to Peter Salisbury, who sustained me throughout its writing.

Versions of some of these poems have appeared in various magazines and journals, including *Poetry Ireland Review*, *New Writing*, *Borderlines*, *Éire/Ireland* and *Sand*.

I am the blind woman finding her way home by a map of tune.
When the song that is in me is the song I hear from the world
I'll be home. It's not written down and I don't remember the words.
I know when I hear it I'll have made it myself. I'll be home.

Paula Meehan, "Home", *Pillow Talk* (1994)

Contents

Author's Note

On 24th May, 1854, a young Kilkenny woman, Margaret Butler, and her nine brothers and sisters, set sail from Liverpool for a new life in Australia. They sailed aboard the Lancaster, a 748 ton barque under the captaincy of a Master Gilks. Documentary evidence, in the shape of an archive of letters written, in the main, by Margaret Butler to her relatives in Ireland, and which was later deposited with the National Library, give us a tantalising glimpse of the life the Butlers made for themselves in Australia.

When I first read the transcriptions, it struck me that the letters were bursting with narrative energy. They paint a clear and vibrant picture of a middle class, prosperous family leaving Ireland because they wished to make a new life in a new country, not because they were forced out of their old one, and who made a highly successful transition in Australia. They were thus very far from the stereotypical image of transported convicts or evicted tenants which we have come to associate with stories of Irish emigration to the Southern Hemisphere. It seemed to me that the Butler archive, which demonstrates very different experiences and preoccupations from those of evicted tenants or failed rebels, offered the potential for inspiring a creative work that would provide an original take on the emigrant experience.

What follows then is a work of fiction. Although I have used extracts from the Butler letters where necessary, I have also invented entirely new letters, or adapted the original ones, where the plot required it. I have also created a cast of fictional characters whose lives, contemporary and historic, intertwine with those of the Butler family. Some of the events described in these pages did happen, others are pure invention, others still a blend of both. I will leave it to the discerning reader to decide which is which.

Dublin, May 2009

Preface

Is this the best place to start?
Here, in the gloom
of a stranger's living room,
in the breath-misting chill
of early January?

Books piled high,
dust everywhere.
Somebody's home,
though it had been months
since a curtain was drawn,
a light was switched on,
the radio played
the one o'clock news.

Was it here, or earlier;
when I picked up the phone,
or when I logged on
and my new life
began to download?

Chapter 1

The Beginning

The best New Year's Eve yet. I slept from 8pm to 6am, missing the bells, the yells and all the false promises that wouldn't make it past noon. I warmed the coffee up, took the last slice of Christmas cake from the wrapper and sat down with telly pages and a plan to do absolutely nothing on this first day of 2003.

Nick and Nora had just got their man when the phone rang and a voice I vaguely knew announced she was in town. Roisin Ryan! It must be 10 years since I'd seen her last, drunk in the upstairs lounge of Nearys. Roisin's been away. First New York, then Santa Fe; now she owns a small boutique in Greenwich Village.

It seemed she'd kept track of me, bought my few pamphlets, always boasted that she knew the bard of Ballyboden when we were in pig-tails. Exaggeration, unless Belfield fashions weren't quite as I remembered them.

She was home to see her folks, and pay her last respects to a great aunt who'd died recently. There were last effects to sort through; did I fancy a trip to Kilkenny to help with the house clearance? 'It'll be a laugh – plenty of time to catch up, down a few pints, compare notes on all those bastards we've been dating.'

It seems Roisin's Auntie was a literary type; there could be first editions to tempt me and there was nothing better lined up until I took that wee trip I was thinking about. But that could wait. So I agreed to meet her on January sixth – *Nollaig na mBan* – Women's Christmas, no less.

* * *

I'd have known her anywhere. It might have been ten years but that Isabella Rosselini bob, babushka doll cheeks and startled blue eyes were unmistakable. Beautiful skin (which moisturiser?) and gravity hadn't begun to play the tricks it pestered me with. She had a prosperous air; wore silk, amber in great chunks at her neck, Choo-shoes, naturally.

We drove to Kilkenny in her car, a rental with more va-va-voom than mine, CD-player belting out Coltrane along the N9. She talked of marriages gone wrong, of New York life and whether I knew what happened to other college pals.

Flash-back to '91: she'd called over once, broken-hearted from the latest escapade, and spent the whole day playing Sinead O'Connor's 'Nothing compares 2 U' over and over till I thought my mother's cassette deck would melt. *It's been seven hours and fifteen days.* Not quite that long in my case, and I hadn't been playing tapes, so I decided to wait a while before telling her about my latest fiasco.

* * *

You'd need an OS map to find Pleaberstown. Roisin hadn't visited since she was a kid but knew the way since the funeral. There wasn't even one horse, just a grocery store, a straggle of two-storeys and a cottage, pebble-dashed, set apart from the others, looking like the kindest thing would be to bull-doze it.

Roisin was apologetic: "Not much to look at, Fiona, and probably fusty inside but who knows what riches we'll find". She turned the yale key in the door and pushed the reluctant wood. We were greeted by dead air, a smell of distant cabbage dinners and old lavender. Gloom inside, dust covering brown furniture though the place was neat, lace doilies dotted here and there by the house-proud auntie who'd seen her last days out in the local Home.

Books everywhere, on shelves, tottering in piles on the floor, leather-bound and paper-back mixed indiscriminately with bundles of newspapers, occasional sheets of writing paper, nice stock, sloped handwriting of another age; her auntie took notes of her reading. We spent the last hours of January light sorting through the debris of a woman's life.

* * *

We agreed to split up; Roisin tackled the bedroom – I didn't feel right in her auntie's sanctum – while I sifted through the living room, setting aside the books of any value though there were no first editions to tempt me. Had her aunt lived in Australia? There were history books, old prints and maps of the continent, tales of travellers and convicts. I wondered if Roisin had relations there; I didn't recall her mentioning any.

She emerged with a Clerys bag full to the brim with papers and photographs "I'll keep these for Mam, but are these of interest?" She handed me a bulging jiffy bag, ribbon-tied, the envelope scrawled with names and dates I couldn't decipher. "Oh it's nothing of worth. Just letters: they look old. Must be from some cousin of auntie's. You take them, Fiona. You're the writer. They're more in your line than mine and if you find a map for buried treasure we can divide out the spoils". She shivered theatrically. "Come on, we've done our bit, it's getting dark and we've pints and steak waiting." The parcel was a snug fit in my shoulder-bag. I'd make space for it later.

* * *

The clock radio blinked 3am in the dusk of the hotel room as a light from the corridor sneaked under the door and sent a heat-seeking dart to the centre of my head. The room didn't swim exactly but I'd had three too many downstairs, had forgotten the hollow legs of my college friend, and made the stupid mistake of trying to keep up with her.

We both retired at twelve, she in company (a five-o'clock shadow-type), me resigned to a fitful sleep solo, but the rogue light and the jiffy bag on the floor had other things in mind.

I emptied its contents out on the salmon-pink shag pile, counted some 50 sheets of closely-printed writing, letters slanted at 90 degrees, lines criss-crossing so the effort to read made me more sea-sick than four gins and tonic had. But I soldiered on, ordered them by date. Sleep seemed aeons away; I'd forgotten my pulp fiction.

Chapter 2

Meeting the Butlers

Pleaberstown
20th March 1845

Dearest Forristal

The matter is at an end. Edward and Father spoke with me last night after supper. They agree that even if the bishop would consent to drop his objections to the match, they could not agree.

With Father on his own I might have found a way – he is so easily persuaded – but once Edward sets his face against something, there is no hope.

We cannot always understand God's purpose for us, though the passing years may make that more clear.

So we must part, dear love. This is the last time I will call you that, although I pray that we will remain the best and most constant of friends.

Your loving Margaret

Pleaberstown
19th November 1845

Cousin

Harsh words I had expected, but the bitterness with which you last wrote has hurt me deeply.

You charge me with many faults, dear cousin, not the least being insincerity and weakness of character. How can I answer that? Must I answer that to someone who I thought knew me better than I knew myself?

I am not too easily led, nor do I give my father or my brother more than their due reverence. They have more experience of the world than I do and have had reason to know how harshly it treats those who flout its conventions. My poor father's recent travails are proof of that.

How many nights have I knelt and sought Our Lord's guidance? Too many to count. But not even prayer would be a consolation if you turned away from me, dear friend.

I have searched my conscience and feel sure it is for the best. In time, you will come to understand and share my faith. Then we can meet again as fondest of cousins, best of friends. Ballyogan will always be my second home, as Pleaberstown is yours.

Fondest regards to Aunt Ansty,

Margaret

Pleaberstown
6 August 1849

Dear Cousin Forristal

As you see, I am safely arrived home at Pleaberstown. The trip from Ballyogan was without incident, except for one broken wheel at Fairley Cross which was soon mended. Edward and I spent the time quite happily, relating all the pleasant events that had passed during our visit. The landscape was quite unspoiled and, thank god, there was little sign of the hunger that is bedevilling other parts of our dear land.

How to convey my heartfelt thanks for all your kindness? You know only too well how grateful I am for your friendship, and for Bessy's too, of course. We are all pleased to see you so well settled and happy.

And pass on our dearest dearest love to Aunt Ansty. She has been like a mother to us all since our own dear parent died. I and my brothers and sisters all agree that wherever we might roam around this world, home would always be with you and dear Ansty.

Wherever we roam! Things are still so uncertain here. It seems Father has resumed his errant ways and is drawn more and more into bad company. Edward is quite afraid about the state of things; he is sure that Father has compromised the lease and he looks very grave each time he comes back from his talks with the Agent.

So we may have to give this dear place up. Where would we go? What would happen to all of us, particularly the little ones? I fear so much for poor Joseph. I have tried to take Mother's place but I know he feels the lack.

Still, my dear cousin, in my mind's eye I can see your dear dear face and that brings consolation. I will not worry until all the facts are known.

Edward and I unite in expressions of regard to you and Bessy, and Aunt Ansty,

Your fond cousin,
Margaret Butler

Camden Street
9 September 1849

Dear Forristal

We must either buy or quit. Affairs being as they are, it would be mad to throw good money after bad and stay at Pleaberstown. The old man let the property get so into debt, the land's not worth the hard-rent, not within 2s-6d an acre of being worth it.

I could buy it out within the half-year – I am the match of Duffy's machinations and could teach Squireen McGrath a thing or two – but think we need a fresh start and now should look around for opportunities. The boys are growing fast; there's nothing for them here, just demagogues and petty rivalries. I have heard good reports of the new colonies. Land is cheap and the Butlers could make their mark in New South Wales.

And as for Father, it would be better to remove him once and for all from the source of the mischief or he'll bring ruin on all our heads.

Margaret is in agreement with me on this although she's fond of the old place and would stay on if let. Advise her, cousin. She has always listened to you.

Love to Bessy and the little one.

Edward

Pleaberstown
May 4th 1850

Dearest Forristal

Thank you for your letter of April 30th which was so welcome. I fully understand you are not so free to visit now that the little ones take up your time and that is how it should be. You have your home, and obligations.

My sisters often tease me that I am of an age to make a match and find myself a home. But since Mother died and Father left it is all that I can do to keep us all together. In truth, it is hard to imagine that any other place might compare in comfort or warmth to what I have known here and with you at Ballyogan. With all my responsibilities, I no longer think of marrying.

Although things seem so perilous now, still I have a sense that I belong here, despite all Edward's talk of joining Father overseas, and taking our chances in a New World. Home is where those you love are and here I'll stay, if they let me.

The girls are all well (Eliza gets bonnier each day, Bridget is still the sensible one, Kate the dreamer) and my brothers are growing into young men, particularly my little pet, Joseph, who has, I think sometimes, a look of you, dear cousin.

All of them unite with me in expressions of fond regard to you, Bessy, Aunt Ansty and the little ones,

Margaret Butler

CHAPTER 3

Extracts from Fiona Sheehan's journal 8th January 2003

Home?

For 30 years a suburban semi-d,
pebble-dashed, walled
in by concrete

I'd play out my fantasies
in the back garden, a crew-cut
Scheherazade in cast-down shorts,
shaded from the cruel desert sun
by Foxford rugs
thrown over upturned chairs.

I spun my tales to blasé Crolly dolls,
though I didn't know then
what fate I must postpone,
got a glimpse of that later
in the street politics
of dodge ball and kick the can.

The lesson quickly learned:
I would always be
a dab hand at spectator sports.

At 31 I bought my own four walls,
eschewed pebble dash for white wash,
chose orchid stems and Persian rugs,
waited for Shahriyar to find the 'burbs.

Margaret 1

Back from Ballyogan
all is resolved
and at an end
Edward says
for the best
consanguinity
they say
cousins
cannot comfort
I am too tired
to gainsay
F says
nothing
a chill takes hold
I feel my head fill
my ears close
their lips move
and I hear
nothing
I want to

Note to Self.
This could make a
cycle of poems…
A woman alone,
others deciding her
fate. I need to find
her a voice.

Margaret 2

the house still
all in bed save me
the last to ascend
the stairs
each night I go
from room to room
plump cushions
extinguish lamps
damp down the fire
ensure all is as was
when the others wake
a slight ache
I cough as
I say my prayers
turn back the sheets
flinch at their cold touch
listen to the wind rise
bring the last leaves
down

Margaret 3

Joseph is sleeping
he curls into himself
too large now
for the cot
too small still
for this man's bed
they have built for him
his poor shape seems
lost in the blankets
he tosses to the floor
if we go he will grow up
in a land
I cannot yet name
cannot describe
I will give him names
for strange trees
I will teach him
to say his prayers
under strange stars

Punctuation non-existent line breaks all wrong, will sort later.

The handwriting's vile and I'm sure I've missed lots without transcription.

I'll take my time.
I need distracting from my own storyline.

CHAPTER 4

The inevitable flashback

I

Or was this the start?

Switching on, clicking the link,
opening new mail after days of silence.

Luke was home
for Christmas,
busy with family, no time
for goodnight darlings,
for reassurance that he was coming
back to Ireland, back to me.

Words lifted off the screen,
cursor flickering to confirm
what my gut had known for weeks.

'Dear Fiona (*or was that Dear Joan?*)
I care for someone else.
I respect you too much to lie.'

Respect was one word for it –
I could think of others
as I went through the Outlook folder,
selecting his name, erasing all trace,
preparing to face my family
for the festivities as familiar lonely heart.

What a prick! His technique
broke my back;
no loss there.

II

I should have scarpered when
he told me he was into NLP;
how else explain such a lapse
than to say I was hypnotised,

a three-month trance, a blind eye
(or two) to his little preferences,
the dirty cartoons in the spare room,
the fairy lights strung up over the camp bed,
his penchant for raw meat …

and yet … and yet …
the thrill of logging on,
the blinking icon, the zing of text.

Why did I waste my time?
I clearly thought it was
a renewable resource.

III

My first love?
Since you ask, William Powell
in the *Thin Man*.

His wisecracks were
the epitome of style, I'd insist
my future man must share his wit.

No dark masters for me;
I scorned my schoolmates' whims
for Darcy or Rochester.

My grandmother said
"For every old sock an old shoe"
and I knew there was one to fit.

Years passed;
I watched my friends pair off,
had vodka-fuelled chats

about what signals
I was sending out
(or wasn't).

Then I fell for the first time
(if you don't count the boy who fenced
and turned out to be gay)

for a beautiful youth,
all gangling limbs and joints that cracked,
eyes like melted Bournville.

But he wouldn't be untrue
to his college sweetheart and by now
I could do platonic pretty well.

My specialist subject
to be the confidante
to a variety of males.

Then sex appeared in the guise
of a curly-haired satyr
who made it look so easy,

gave me a taste for Sundays in bed
and moonlight dances
and doing it on beaches.

My mistake was to think
it would out-last
the novelty.

But I was finally launched,
could look my friends in the eye,
trade stories about male perfidy.

The pattern was set,
the search and find, the rescue
when it all went wrong,

as it always did.
There was no other way, the happy ones
were just fooling themselves.

When my father stopped asking had I met
anyone I cared for more than myself,
I knew my fate was set.

IV

Christmas morning I woke
in my own house,
my own bed.

The air quiet, families in the estate
not moving yet, too early for
the boot-slamming exodus to the parents'.

There was frost; bamboo grass petrified,
the beech-hedge frozen and glistening,
a wren rifling through bark chip.

A trace of the morning star as the sun
began its slow arc from the firs
by the Owen Dower to the giant walnut tree,

warming roof tiles,
revealing terracotta red
little by little.

It was warm inside, a gas-fired cosy glow
to swan about in, sip coffee, to open gifts,
no wise man to wrestle the remote from.

There was no need yet to pack my overnight,
to don the face of daughter, sister,
peace-maker, bottle-washer.

No need for mistletoe or angel's bells
until I drove my grudging way
to Bedford Falls.

V

I arrived to a full house,
crammed to the brim
with forced smiles,
children rushing round
glucose-charged
from room to room,
adults surreptitiously
checking their watches -
(the marrieds that is -
we spinsters knew
we were there for the long haul;
nobody to go home to, after all.)

So time could suspend itself,
go backwards, Scrooge-like,
though Christmas Pasts
were just the same
as this one, the same vow
that next year would be different.

The kitchen full, I drifted to the living room
where a sister-in-law eyed me warily,
never quite sure what note to strike
with the writer in the family.

Small talk exhausted, she turned to poetry.
'There's a new book out', she said brightly,
'I heard it on *The Pat Kenny Show*.
Everyone's in it.
Are you?'

Terrific! I'd hoped the latest oversight
would go un-noticed, they don't usually
give a toss about my scribblings.

'I'm not in that one, just an editor
who doesn't know her arts from her elbow,'
I laughed convincingly.

Did I imagine that the room went quiet,
did several pairs of eyes look away?
Christmas makes you paranoid!

VI

I sleep-walked through Stephen's Day.
A night in a single bed and mallow-soft
mattress had left me aching
and from the mood
in the living room
no-one had slept well.

Dad was already installed,
flicking through channels
like a man possessed,
Mother was tidying, muttering
under breath as she crunched
discarded wrappers into tight balls.

'Your sister's already left. Couldn't wait
to get away, had friends to visit, apparently.'
'Friends' pronounced venomously.
Wise move, I thought,
and wondered how to devise
my exit strategy.

My eye fell to the floor,
to a colour brochure a niece
had shoved under the sofa.
I pulled it out, took a note
of the special New Year offer
with some ferry line to the UK.

Not a bad deal.
Maybe a one-way trip
was just what the head-doctor ordered.

VII

Awkward moment in the hall.
I thought I'd slip out while
the others were taking their leave
so I grabbed my overnighter,
had just pulled back the door
when my father emerged.

He took it all in: the bag, the covert exit.
"Your mother and I had hoped
you'd stay a while longer.
We see you so rarely these days.
Could you not take your ease,
have a cup in your hand with us?"

He smiled tentatively. I swallowed.
There was time, after all.
"Sorry, Dad. I'm expecting a call."

VIII

The third G&T did it.
I sat in the snug in Keoghs
with the usual crowd of hacks and poets
(who was it said, *hyenas scrabbling for scraps?*),
listening for the umpteenth
to some diatribe about the latest literary comet.

I was ready with my cracks
about casting couch publishers
and how it was all a fad
and nobody cared
for real writing nowadays
when I heard that bitter tone
and thought my mother
had shown up suddenly
and was letting us have it.

How had it come to that?
Promising novice into also-ran
without my noticing.

Back home I checked my email.
Still no more word from Luke
though countless offers to boost my manhood.

I leafed through a pile of books.
No more than 30 poems for a decade's work.
I pulled out my suitcase.

CHAPTER 5

Orphan

Loughrea Workhouse,
September 1847

I wasn't born here,
but don't remember any other home.
Ma brought us in one winter
when our stomachs got too loud,
she died soon after.

Then it was just me.

We live behind high white walls,
sleep in cattle stalls.
I only left once,
tried out at a farmer's house
where I cooked, scrubbed –
they sent me back
as I didn't please the mistress.

Each day the same.
Up before cock crow,
we rake our straw,
dry-rub the walls
till they shine,
then kneel two hours
in the prayer hall.

If God hears, he doesn't let on.

We queue for oatmeal
and watered-milk,
we do our shift –
steeping shirts, spinning flax,

only the infants and dying
have no work.

Once the laundry was short
some scraps of cloth –
we were taken out,
one by one, and searched.
The men watched,
low laughs behind hands.

Some devil urged me on
and I spoke up,
said they had no right
to treat us so barbarous.

Quick as anything I was caught,
dragged out by the hair.
The Master pulled at my clothes,
left my breast bare.
He kicked me, dragged me,
put his hands
where he shouldn't have

till the girls gathered around,
nudging like young calves
closer and closer
so he had to turn, go back
to where the men stood laughing.

The girls lifted me, covered me up,
found a rag to stop the blood,
carried me to the corner
of the woman's yard.

But they came
and searched me there,
lifting up my skirt,
reckoning what I wore.

I had but one petticoat.

Loughrea Workhouse,
March 1849

I was no troublemaker.
I did my chores, said my prayers,
kept my eyes down when the Master passed
but he had marked me that day.

So when he called me into his office
I thought the worst,
was surprised at his polite voice
that he bade me sit.

I saw the Guardian in the corner,
and with him a man in naval uniform,
a doctor with a kind look.

They were drawing up a list.
Had I ever heard tell of Australia?
I said I was not sure,
but thought it pretty far.

The doctor examined me,
asked about illnesses,
then said I was fit to travel.

The Guardian said it was a decent trip
and wouldn't I like to see Australia for myself?

I caught the Master's look and said yes.

Plymouth,
23rd October 1849

The word has gone round the Depot.
Tomorrow we set sail
and put an end to all this waiting.
Not that we mind the wait.
The room is clean,
there are fewer girls
and food is regular.

We each have our own trunks,
names painted on the front,
a list of contents underneath the lid -
six shifts, two petticoats,
six pairs of stockings,
shoes and two warm gowns,
a prayer-book and a bible.

We keep the trunks locked.

We were examined again today.
Another doctor who
will sail with us.
He showed us more respect
than others have.
He checked our heads,
ordered warm baths and haircuts.

Tonight I said my prayers
but cannot sleep for the excitement.
Other girls are weeping
but not I.
I have left no-one behind.
God willing, there will be more chances
in a new world where
nobody goes hungry or dies.

The word feels strange
on my tongue
but I like the sound,
Aus –tray –lee-ah.

CHAPTER 6

Getaway

I

A quiet stroll around town and the Sales:
Grafton Street jammed with harpies in jimmy choos,
hefting bags twice their body size
but everywhere else seemed empty.

I walked towards Merrion Square,
passed the Shelbourne with its party-over air,
nodded to the graves
in the Huguenot cemetery
(too early for Hartnett's bluebells)
and meditated on the prospect
of hot chocolate at the Gallery
with other Christmas refugees.

But before that, one more chore.
The ferry company had offices here,
which were open despite the holidays,
ready to do business with anyone
looking to get away for a while,
a short break or long haul.

Surprisingly, no queues! I wandered inside
and within five minutes had emerged
clutching a one-way ticket – my exit pass.

II

I've only just learned
that you're only as big
as the ones who take your calls.

You can measure your size
by the length of the gap
between the *can I help you?*
twang of an anonymous blonde –
chewing gum, copy of 'Take a Break'
open at the horoscope -

and the cold reconnect, the pat lines,
the *not at her desk right now,*
at a meeting, can she call you back?

And you swallow the gorge of
I didn't get where I am today without ...
Meek as you like,
because you have to play this game,
you can't afford to take
or give offence

or she'll remember, put you on hold,
next time, placed in a queue,
your call is important to us,
a constant loop
of waiting and waiting
for someone, somewhere, to ring.

III

Two weeks later
and I still hadn't mentioned
I was planning a trip,
but that ticket was now burning a hole
and if I really wanted to stay away
I'd have to make arrangements,

tell the folks,
say goodbye to my mates
(would they notice?)
look for tenants for the house,
not to mention find a job, some way
to support this mad endeavour.

Or should I just abandon the notion?
Things weren't that bad, and the legion
of devils I knew were better than ...?

I picked up the pack of letters
I'd been flicking through
for the past few days.
Although the writing was faint,
the slanting scrawl near illegible
I could still glean some of their meaning.

CHAPTER 7

An Emigrant's Preparation

Pleaberstown
13 September 1852

My dearest Forristal

It was well you had an early start and escaped the tremendous rain. All day the skies grew dark till by four we had the candles lit throughout the house. Eliza and I sat in the parlour looking out the old bay as the first drops splashed the glass and the wind picked up and shook the branches and leaves were whipped off and came flying through the air.

Bridget brought four pails and there was need of them when the steady drip began through brown spots in the wood left from last winter. Edward says repair is a needless expense – he seems content to leave this dear place go to rack and ruin now he has turned his thoughts to departure.

I thought Bessy would have set out herself if you had not returned. She'll think twice before allowing you to offer to come again.

Will you write to Dublin for that book? Direct it to be sent to the Station at Thomastown. If, as it seems, we are for new parts, I would like to read and know what I might expect. Perhaps it doesn't rain in Australia! But who will I have to write to, dearest cousin, when I am far away?

My best and warmest love to Bessy and Aunt Ansty and to all the little ones.

Yours always, Margaret

Pleaberstown
22 September 1852

My dearest Forristal

Summer ended with a storm. Last week had promised much, we thought we might stretch the evenings yet, walk to the bridge before supper, smell the after-breath of roses, the night-scented stock that Edward brought from Ballyogan. Do you recall that flower? So sweet on the night air, yet in the day withdrawn to bud, withered and homely as a weed. It won't have survived the deluge.

Eliza says she loves the longer nights. She bustles around, lighting lamps, placing logs just so around the hearth. But I am sad when evenings draw in, I shiver in the gloom, turn my thoughts to long ago – the warm parlours, sing-songs and games of cards with my dear friend. All <u>distant</u> and <u>past</u>, all that is left are <u>kind</u> <u>kind</u> remembrances. And letters, which soon may have to travel across the world to reach the ones I love. Will you still remember your fondest of correspondents?

There is still no word from Father, who does not write, but Mrs Morris has heard from her son in Sydney that he has got a place. You would think that he might let us know his address.

Forgive my ravings, dear cousin. I may have caught a chill in the downpour. Give my fond regards to B. and all the little ones, especially the Duck Man (does he grow tall?),

yours, Margaret

Pleaberstown
2 November 1852

Dear Forristal,

Mr Egan has forwarded the book. The station-master sent that it had come so William was dispatched to Thomastown post-haste. We've been poring over its pages since he came back. Such a small book to describe a new world.

It's hard to take it all in. The country is <u>2,000</u> <u>miles</u> East to West and <u>1,700</u> from North to South. Eliza asked how many County Kilkennys that would fit and though the Chambers Guide is quite exact it could not answer that!

But how we gasped about the things portrayed: the vast landscapes, mountains, shattered peaks; rivers that go for miles and flood betimes while others are mere trickles; sparse interiors that they call bush; and parklands which the manual said could match any gentleman's estate in England. Edward laughed at that, he likes the notion of being an Australian gentleman. Michael prefers the farmer's life, his eyes grew wide at mention of 10 million sheep that graze the country's pastures.

I liked less the other beasts it mentioned. Animals with pouches called kangaroos that are five feet tall, leap twenty feet and can outstrip a horse on occasion. Others things called opossums and, would you credit it, a thing half-bird, half-beast with a duck's bill and feet, but with the body of a rat. And rivers full of <u>every</u> <u>type</u> of fish, and shrimps and mussels of the kind Edward eats in those fancy Dublin restaurants. But snakes, can you believe? These colonists had not the benefit of St. Patrick's prayers.

The thing that worried me most were the native folk. Aborigines they're called, jet black, the book says, with 'large heads, large lips and wide mouths, and are altogether the reverse of beautiful'. It says they are amongst 'the lowest of all known savages in the scale of intellect.' William growled at that, saying it reminded him of *Punch* or *London Illustrated* scenes of Ireland; that nearly caused a fight with Edward! But I don't know what to think, and only pray we won't have much dealings with their kind.

At least the climate promises better things, even if the seasons are reversed. The guide says people live to greater age, there is a woman of 125 who is still working in the fields, children grow taller and the dry air is good for consumptives. I'm sure Kate will thrive in those conditions. It seems New South Wales is the jewel in the Colony's crown. Land is much easier to get and there are generous deals for those with capital. Edward is sanguine that we will all make a better life for ourselves. The boys, of course, can think of nothing but the gold that's being found over there.

So it seems we're off by no later than the Spring of '54, once Edward gets our affairs in order. There is so much to do. I must be prepared.

your cousin, Margaret Butler

CHAPTER 8

Extracts from Fiona Sheehan's journal 24th January 2003

Why bother to find
a precise name for the pain
beneath my bottom rib?

Prosaic causes for complaint:
the sky dappled the wrong hue,
the moon too slow,
the to-ing and fro-ing
on the stairs,

laughter next door
a prelude to throes
passionate as clockwork.

Across the wall,
hostile screams.
Familiar contempt is better
than this quiet room,
waiting for tears to well
to Barber's predictable strings.

Margaret 4

Still haven't found a form, work on the voice for now

Each night the same
I wake in the dark
breath short
the dream
at the edge
of memory
birds still quiet
too early to rise
too early to rouse
the house
my chest pains me,
there is a pressure
at the back of my eyes
I feel my heart's
dull rhythm
and I fear
what I'll feel
when my feet
touch the floor

Margaret 5

Father goes ahead
he set his mind to it
for once could not
be shifted from
his strange course
to Lord knows where
Edward mutters
about creditors
their reach being
not long enough
What I want to ask
I cannot
Will our ties

stretch that far
will he wait
for us to find him
on the other side

Margaret 6

Nightmare
again
the same face
black as Satan
red eyes
lips bared
a snake
round his waist
at his feet
a beast with
a dog's head
bird's wings
a moon
huge and
blank
curving
a wrong
arc

CHAPTER 9

The Leaving of Dublin

I

It was simple in the end.
I found a small ad,
a company in North Wales
looking for editors.
I could do that with one hand
tied behind my keyboard.

Maybe the poems would come back
in a new landscape where people
didn't keep track of a poor record,
where nobody would ask,
"How's yer man?" and gurn that
'no surprise there' smile I hated.

And Wales was close to home,
a two-hour ferry ride
if it didn't work out.

I found a letting agent, slick, red-haired,
agreed a price and handed over
a set of house keys,
began the task
of boxing up my life
into carboot-size chunks.

II

Extract from Fiona Sheehan's journal
26th January 2003

These walls unhouse me,
magnolia paint smoothing away
the scrapes of nine years,
unwary scuffs with trays,
finger marks of
occasional passion.

Dry-cleaned curtains preen,
patterns freed from nicotine,
carpet fluffed, innocent of wine spills,
of coffee cups, though a ring
betrays the sheen
of the dining room table.

The garden wears its Sunday best –
waiting for other guests
to light candles in it,
to smell the lavender,
cut rosemary for lamb roasts,
watch the slow growth of crab-apples.

I close the door, hear the Chubb click
the ending of this conversation,
or the pause ...

III

The ship slipped past containers;
snow sprinkling the Sugar Loaf
my last view of home.

The crew were all polite but bored.
I arranged my bags, grabbed
port-side windows

and eyed the clock,
waiting for the buffet to open, to while
away the hours with indigestible food.

It was an accident when I cuffed the child
running past me for the umpteenth;
her parents in the bar, presumably.

Feedback turned our heads:
a blonde singer was setting up
in the passenger lounge.

Her backing track brought
Vegas to the Irish Sea,
her banter mid-Atlantic.

Second hour up, the crowd stirred.
The sky changed, horizon taking shape
as mobiles beeped,

announced new ways to keep in touch
with Wales opening up
its snag-tooth smile.

IV

I needed somewhere to live.
The papers listed names,
unpronounceable places,
with occasional photographs of
grey terraces, grey stone.

Visits to each place
took me up vertiginous slopes,
challenging my car with corkscrew
bends at right-angles.

I was surrounded by slate,
beech trees hanging over dripping walls,
hard-faced houses clinging to mountains.

Then a lucky break.
There was a house on Anglesey,
looking over at hills, not dwarfed by them.
I liked the name: Beaumaris.
Promises of fine sea views,
Victorian promenades.

Extract from Fiona Sheehan's journal
29th January 2003

i

Not so hard, then.
A short ferry ride,
some forms to fill,
helplines to register
a fresh existence
in a strange town.

Now, sofa-stretched,
TV lip-synched, sleep-
settling to a stiff neck at 1am.

I am what I choose.
Possibilities persist
until the morning.

ii

I'll get a cat.
We'll watch the night fall,
comatose with deluxe dining
on Whiskas and readymeals.

We'll curl up on the sofa,
gasp at reality shows, purr
at the twinkle in the chat-host's eye.

Later, we'll go out hunting,
scouring the undergrowth
on the wild side of Henllys,
navigate silky trails,
breathe in the damp dusk
till our pores ooze musk.

She'll show me the dark delight
of fur and sinew, the oh so
delicate crunch of back-bone.

31st January

Some days I wake
and wonder where
I've washed up.

The tide's gone out,
yachts lie where they fell,
tilted awkwardly on props.

Motor boat engines
clench black fists in air, stranded
by a breeze withholding forecasts.

On the sand-bar
shadows search for pickings,
fill their bags, move on.

Closer to shore clockwork
oyster-catchers bob, then take to air
as a radio pips noon.

A black-backed gull
pulls at something
long-tailed.

A car kerb-crawls
for a spot on the sea-front,
fails, resumes the circuit.

I watch a man walk his dog, pause,
read the sign he has seen
every day for a lifetime.

CHAPTER 10

Voyager

I do not know the date.
Hours go into days
go into weeks.
Each morning the same.
We wake to blackness,
the only light
the glow of Matron's lantern.

But our nostrils fill:
oak tar mixed with sweat,
damp wool, the tang
of vegetables on the turn,
sometimes a hint of rum,
always animal dung.

And there are a hundred sounds:
creaking wood,
the muffled thump of water,
the hoarse shouts of crewmen;
the groans and sighs
of 200 girls dreaming of home.

Some dream of the place
we are going to,
and wake up screaming,
telling of tigers and elephants
and burning trees
and savages with red bloody eyes.

I dream of water:
green swamps I wade through,
fronds cloak my skin,
huge foamy waves
lifting me high up.

I'm never afraid.
I find my feet, stride on,
always wake before
I reach the end of water.

Off the Cape of Good Hope,
25th December, 1849

A strange Christmas.
I woke early and came on deck
to find the sea quite flat,
a grey mist settling around the masts
like an old shawl.
The deck was wet –
planks cold beneath my feet.

All was quiet save the caoin of the seabirds;
they sounded as mournful
as the girls last night,
who'd sat about crying for Ireland
and blaming fate
for abandoning them to exile.

Doctor Strutt tried to hush them up,
said there'd be no Christmas dinner
if they didn't quiet.
Later they filed in small groups
to the upper deck at midnight
to where the priest said mass for us.

Today the Captain called us all at half past twelve.
There was mutton and spuds and buttermilk,
plum pudding, dark and juicy it was
and so rich I thought I'd never swallow it.
The doctor gave each girl
a glass of punch to help it settle.

Then we sang carols
and the younger ones
danced with the crewmen –
the Captain turned a blind eye
for the night that was in it.

A ship's mate said the seasons
are different in Australia,
that summer's in December and
Christmas falls in hot, dry weather.
I liked the sound of that
but all the same joined with the rest
and sang old songs
of frosty nights and snowy cribs,
raised a toast to Ireland in our wake.

Female Immigrant Depot, Macquarie Street,
10th February 1850

Two days on Australian soil
and it seems we've swapped
one set of high walls for another.

Convicts were held in this place
and they have kept the iron bars
to lock us in for fear
we'd terrorise the locals
with our wild Irish ways.

The day we arrived some men came
and took their pick of us
for serving girls or housekeepers.
They looked us up and down,
inspected teeth and gums,
inquired about fleas and lice,
talked above us like we couldn't hear!

A few got jobs,
the rest of us must bide.
We have heard of work
in a small town south of here
where they raise sheep
and other Irish live.

It is a three-day trip
through bush
but I will risk it.
I yearn for open space,
for sun and low walls.

Macquarie Street
10 March 1850

Delay after delay.
Each day they promise
that we'll leave tomorrow
but we gather at dawn,
bags in hand,

only to wait for another
shamefaced excuse:
the horses are lame,
a broken wheel,
a flash flood along the trail
that washed away the road.

I swear they hope
we'll just disappear,
one by one, into
this dusty town
where men stand at corners,
watching us over their pipes,
farmers eyeing
a side of beef
at a cattle mart.

The few women here:
shadows who keep
their glance down,
slip into doorways
when we pass,
vanish like ghosts.

Depot, Macquarie Street
17 March 1850

Still here on the saint's day
so a little feast was planned.
The doctor made punch,
but Matron glared,
waiting for the least sign
that we girls were the loose type
the whispers said we were.

Later a few of us slipped out,
walked the dark streets,
breathed the warm air,
talking about how this time last year
the snow froze the shamrock
growing round the walls of Loughrea.

Down at the seamen's guild
the smell of spirits and beer
spilled out through the open windows.
Inside we saw rows of men,
heads down, chins to their chests,
clutching glasses to their breasts,
each man more silent than the next
till notes rose from the corner of the room,

the reedy sound of a mouth organ
offering a Hail Glorious Saint Patrick
which was taken up, one by one,
till the whole room bellowed it
out through the windows,
down the street,
the tune winding
round the masts
in the Harbour.

CHAPTER 11

Getting down to work

I

Another email from Roisin,
full of the joys of a New York spring
and the latest squeeze.

She asked about the move,
was I settled in, had I got
anywhere with the letters yet?

I didn't really feel
like telling her my progress,
sharing my plans for poems,
the book, the radio documentary.
Another fascinating insight
into the mind of an émigré.

Something that could get me
back into the spot-light.
Time enough to tell that –

I had work to do.
There was no faster way
than transcribe, word by word,
leave the gaps, just hope
the meaning would emerge
when I pieced it together.

II

This lot could take years!
Each letter a mass of ink-stained
runes, blotchy and worn.

But slowly a picture emerged,
dot by dot, stroke by stroke,
like black and white film in developing fluid.

I could hear Margaret's voice, a tone
that I thought I recognised;
someone who lost the fight to stay at home.

It reminded me of a college trip
Roisin and I once took to visit
her émigré sister with a flat in Paris.

Ciara nearly threw us out
after a post-dinner row when I, in my cups,
claimed she hadn't had the mettle to stay in Dublin.

A funny thing. Ciara is now ensconced
in a family semi-D in Lucan, Roisin and I
scattered to Greenwich Village and Gwynedd.

III

Impatient with my speed,
wanting to know more,
I wondered if some friendly archivist
might lend a hand,

show me the tricks of the trade
how to transform slants and cross-strokes
into courier or times new roman.

I'd take a trip to Bangor
see if a librarian there
might suggest a formula.

IV

Extract from Fiona Sheehan's journal 12th February 2003

The landscape is patient,
permits my slow
discoveries.

I turn a bend,
a buzzard leads me,
wing-span wide enough
to fill the windscreen
as he beats the air,
then sweeps away seawards.

I test out place-names,
my tongue still mutinies over
u's and w's, hellish double ells.

And proof the eye
will fool you:
standing on Mynydd Mawr
looking towards Wicklow
you might be on Bray Head,
looking back at Lleyn.

Someone speaks,
a different music soars,
reminds you that the ground
you stand on is not your own,
though it might
lend itself a while.

The first lambs out,
and it only February.
Here, where I write,
there's a new vase,
the first daffodils
coaxing the sun.

CHAPTER 12

Point of departure

Pleaberstown
5th January 1853

Dearest Forristal

Just a short note to enclose 1s 1d so please send me ¼ of the best tea. Aunt Bessy can bring it when she comes on Wednesday. Tell her I will wait by the bridge.

I can hardly credit some news just received. John Clancy, a young man from the next parish, has written from Australia to say he has work building roads and he reports that our Father is now working as a steward on £2 a day. I think he might have written to let us know. We have been so worried about it but it seems he gives us not a thought.

Perhaps, as Edward says, it will be better for us all when we are all together again in that strange land.

Yours hastily

Margaret

Pleaberstown
25th December 1853

My dearest Forristal

So this is really to be our last Christmas at home! It seems so strange to be celebrating the birth of our Lord while surrounded by packing boxes and white cloth coverings for the furniture. We went to early Mass, then Eliza rustled up quite a feast of goose and dripping and fine fruit pudding. The young ones were full of merriment but I could not find an appetite when we all sat down, much to young Joseph's delight and Eliza's disgust. Joe was very happy to assist in the clearing of my plate! He is growing up so fast and will be quite the young man by the time we arrive in Australia.

We leave for Dublin just after New Year and Edward says everything must be in readiness. We will require two carriages which may prove difficult to secure without the neighbourhood being alerted to our departure – Edward is adamant that we must keep the secret for as long as possible lest the remainder of the creditors descend upon us. He has settled all that he believes honour requires – as for the rest, he declares they are blackguards of the highest order who led Father astray and thus caused the greater part of our difficulties. They have already exacted enough punishment and are welcome to pick among the remains of what we leave behind us at Pleaberstown, which may be a considerable amount, as we can bring so little with us to the new world. So says Edward. But the thought of strangers weighing up our possessions and assaying our worth leaves me feeling sick to the pit of my stomach. But I cannot say this to Edward, or indeed any of the family. They have trepidation enough about the coming journey, without my adding to it.

So my dear dear cousin, I greatly wish that you and Bessy might come between now and New Year and take some keepsakes back to Ballyogan. It still seems impossible that within a matter of weeks I will be heading to the other side of the world and that I am unlikely to see my dearest friends again. I know that we said our goodbyes last week (it was such a joy to hold you all and to lift up my little Duck Man who is now such a weight!) but if you could manage to come just one more time, and stand with me upon the old bridge like we used to do, I would be deeply grateful. There is still so much to do but there is always enough time for dear friends.

We all join in sending our fond love to you and Bessy and Ansty and the little ones

Yours, Margaret Butler

19th March 1854
Liverpool

Dearest Forristal

Here we are, and here we wait a fortnight at least till the tide is right and we set sail for Sydney. Edward secured our berths at 18 guineas each! The price is prohibitive and yet we must ensure we make the voyage in some comfort. 18 guineas buys a cabin for each.

And another guinea each for the voyage over here! We sailed from Howth on St. Patrick's Day (auspicious date for the first leg of our great adventure) on a packet steamer of the Dublin & Liverpool line. When first we boarded I was sure we had mistaken the ship, so great were the number of animals crowding the decks. Cattle, sheep, pigs, all in great noise and confusion with a scattering of men herding them below. The human cargo huddled where they could – steerage passengers finding no space beneath that was not taken up by animals. The poor souls stood, crowded and shivering, for the 14 hours that the boat steamed to Liverpool. But we at least were in reasonable comfort, warm, dry and received a good meal of beef and port wine. None were sick, the steward said the swell was moderate, that we were lucky for this time of year.

But all were glad when Liverpool came in sight, a majestic place of great ships with many masts, white sails gleaming. Huge crowds milled the docks and we were besieged by every kind of man and child trying to prevail upon us with tickets to embark, or maps to boarding houses, offering to take our bags and guide us to select accommodation. Edward soon convinced them that we should be left to walk unmolested.

We found our way to Wapping and Wakeman's Boarding House where Mrs Wakeman was expecting us with welcome cups of tea and cuts of bread. There must be 100 people staying here – such is the throng seeking a new life. We are crowded to the point of suffocation.

I will write again before we leave. Now we must gather provisions to see us through the long journey to a new world. It would be a great service if you could send, if you can, six pounds of tea, some quinine and two gallons of whiskey wrapped in cloth and placed inside a sack of potatoes. Edward asks for 1 lb of snuff.

Tomorrow Edward and I walk out to see our ship, the Lancaster, which is newly arrived and anchored in the harbour. A barque, I'm told, whose captain is Master Gilks. I can hardly believe it will carry me away so many thousands of miles from all I love. I cannot restrain my tears so I will leave off.

All here unite in expressions of regard,
Your loving Margaret

30th June 1854
The Barque Lancaster

Dear Forristal

I had not thought I would be writing to you again till we landed in Australia. We had been five weeks at sea when a steward, a Lyons from Inistioge, would you credit it, informed us that we'd shortly pass a ship heading back for Liverpool and home, so if we wanted to dispatch letters to our loved ones we should make haste. No further encouragement was needed – I think that letters are my life's blood now, the current that will keep me tied to home.

So you will hear all the adventures we have met since setting sail from Liverpool on May 24th. We had waited for two days in the Mersey, after being pulled from Queen's Dock by a steam tug, waiting, waiting, for the winds to lift. Then pandemonium when Master Gilks gave the order to set sail. Sailors manning their posts, climbing masts, untying ropes, and passengers rushing about, setting up a shout and dancing their delight, overjoyed, it seems, to be underway and leaving their homelands for ever.

Someone had brought the union pipes and soon the air was filled with Irish tunes – so like a floating Ireland we became I wondered whether any people were left back home. A veritable Noah's ark we were, too, with cattle, sheep, geese setting up their clamour below decks once the music started.

The first gales blew up as we passed Lambay and the Irish Sea grew wild, losing that mild, calm look that had deceived us. Many of us then recalled the sad fate of the Tayleur. They say 400 souls perished when it was wrecked off Lambay last January, all of them making for a new life in Australia. A sad fate. But those were winter gales — a summer storm or two could not threaten us.

Poor Eliza was the worst for *mal du mer* but all the girls kept to our cabin, and couldn't eat for days, so sick did the motion make us. The boys were all out on deck, yelling with joy at each roll of the ship until the captain told them to go back below. The gales lasted three days – I thought I'd never find my feet again, despaired that we would not have a single piece of uncracked crockery to unload in Australia. Things eased, and Eliza, Mary, Bridget, Kate and I braved the decks on the days when winds were gentle enough.

I can't recall all the strange places we have passed though Edward keeps his journal assiduously and will have a fine account to send you all once landed. I knew the Bay of Biscay for the squalls that sent us back below deck for days but it became clear enough to catch a sight of Madeira off portside (I have learned the sailor's lingo as you see) though it was little more than a speck on the horizon.

We are passing down the coast of Africa presently. Who would have thought during all those nights at Pleaberstown that one day we might cross the Equator? The sailors have a practice for each new recruit when this great event occurs. What it is I cannot tell, as the ladies were all asked to go below before the ritual got under way, but we heard the sounds of much merriment above our heads.

The weather is too hot most days to venture out and we keep below, although it can be stifling and we're forced to brave the glare for an hour so as to fill our lungs with hot, dry air. That's when we catch a glimpse of strange animals. There was quite a furore when turtle fish were spotted — sailors and steerage passengers grabbed pikes and anything they could use to spear them. The meat is very sweet, or so I'm told; Edward could not prevail upon me to try some.

As for food, the rations are quite good on board; we have regular supply of mutton and beef, enough potatoes to keep all satisfied, wine and brandy, and fresh water, though this is guarded as a precious commodity — the Captain keeps buckets out to catch rain-water. Of course the steerage class fare worse than we; I've seen some miserable and thin wraiths scavenging and begging scraps from the sailors' mess. There have also been bouts of sickness — one woman nearly died I believe and others look like they'll hardly survive the journey. My heart goes out to my fellow countrymen.

Boredom is the worst we have to face. Although there is diversion from time to time – some of the passengers delight in tormenting sea-birds with their target practice – the days are all the same, an expanse of grey water, sometimes green, or brown, but rarely blue and never anything for the eye to fix on. The steward says we aren't quite half-way, but promises that it will grow much livelier when we round the Cape and hit what he calls the 'Roaring Forties'.

I must sign off – a shout has gone up that the other ship has been sighted. So I must wish you all a fond fond farewell and send you best wishes from all our crew to you, Aunt Bessie, Ansty and the little ones.

Your loving Margaret

1st October 1854
Sydney

Dear Cousin

We landed safely here on 9th September and are currently settled in lodgings while I make arrangements for the family to obtain permanent accommodation. Temporary lodgings are expensive (a small house costs half a guinea a week for all of us and it seems that merchants take pride in extracting huge premium from newly arrived settlers such as we) but at least it appears easy for reputable men to obtain land. I had received letters from the administration in New South Wales before embarking which assured me a lease of more than 500 acres of good land close to Sydney so I am hopeful that we will secure somewhere soon.

My priorities are for somewhere with good grazing land – Michael is keen to test his husbandry skills – and with a house with ample space for Father, Margaret, and the others. It is my intention to stay in Sydney and I have already made contact with a former colleague from Chambers in Dublin who has given me an introduction to the Chief Justice. Legal professionals are still a rarity here so I am confident I will find an opening within days.

We were in total 15 weeks at sea and a voyage which, while not eventful, was full of incident. We had the good fortune to sail in a well managed ship with a good master and a disciplined crew and thus were spared the sorts of excesses we have heard from some of the other recent arrivals we have met here in Sydney. It appears that it is not unusual for ships to be becalmed and to run low on provisions, which had already been squandered by a corrupt crew – the poorer passengers might face starvation even before they land. But thankfully that was not the case on the Lancaster. Master Gilks kept a firm hand on his crew but was a fair man and he appeared to have equal concern for the welfare of the most important and the lowliest of his passengers. We none of us starved and there was little sickness among the Butlers, apart from a slight discomfort for the girls from time to time.

Our route was as follows: we left Liverpool on 24th May and headed through the Bay of Biscay south past Spain and towards the coast of Africa. We stopped first at Tenerife on 16th of June, where we got fresh supplies and made minor repairs to the ship. We then sailed on to the Cape Verde islands and, after another two weeks, we passed the equatorial line. The crew arranged a ceremony to mark this auspicious event, which they called Crossing the Line. The ladies were invited to go below deck before the festivities got underway. Then the mate, who had assumed the role of Neptune and wore his bay laurels (in fact kelp tied together with ship's rope) with great gravitas, called upon all those who had for the first time crossed the equator, to step forward. There was much nervousness among the five or six young Pollywogs, as they were termed, and much hilarity amongst the other sailors, who knew what lay in store for them. A barrel of water and a bar of soap were produced and a large cut-throat razor was brandished by the boatswain, who was also dressed like some Roman God or other. The Pollywogs were ordered to drop their trousers; those who demurred were manhandled cheerfully by the rest of the crew. However, Master Gilks was careful to ensure that events did not become too boisterous; grog had been carefully rationed on the day in question. The Master later told me that it was a time-honoured ceremony going back to the Vikings. The ladies were quite scandalised when the events were related to them later on, although I did not tell my sisters every detail.

We then continued along the coast of Africa to Cape Town, meeting occasional lapses of wind when we were becalmed but making good progress generally. We reached Cape Town on July 12th, restocked and re-equipped for a week and then departed for the most hazardous and challenging leg of the voyage, the 6,500 miles to Sydney through 'The Roaring

Forties'. July and August are winter months in the southern hemisphere, and so we faced mountainous seas and gales that lasted up to two days a piece. At the height of the bad weather, my sisters stayed below and suffered greatly from *mal du mer*, especially Margaret, who is not robust at the best of times. It was remarkable to watch the industry of the crew at such moments, manning the pumps and repairing whatever damage the treacherous winds caused. But we were never in danger; the Lancaster is a sound ship and she faced her travails with great fortitude. There were great extremes of cold – some crewmen suffered badly from frostbite and seamen in the rigging could not wear gloves lest it hinder their work with the ropes. But we survived these extremities, and arrived into Sydney Cove some two months after leaving Cape Town. Since arriving we have made ourselves quite comfortable in our new country; there are many people here happy to assist new arrivals with good prospects to find their feet.

I shall write again once we have secured a permanent address. I know that Margaret is keen to have all the news from you all. She has been low in spirits since our arrival but I feel sure that once she is mistress of a new home, she will have plenty to distract her.

I send our best wishes and respects to Bessy, Aunt Ansty and the little ones.

Edward Butler

CHAPTER 13

Extract from Fiona Sheehan's journal 18th February 2003

Margaret 7

So she finally went. Poor Mags, her whole world turned upside down.

I did not believe
until now
until the first step off land
and my stomach lurched
with the sway of wood
on water
I did not believe
until now
felt sure
we would
turn back before
finding port
let the horses
retrace the path
to Pleaberstown

Margaret 8

We wait
for tide
I watch
the ebb
the current's
slow tug
pulling us
further
and further

till the rope
must fray
undo
the knot
that binds me

Margaret 9

Dead heat
damp clothes
dead weight
breath
caught
in my ribs
no shift
in sails
Must we stay
in this wood
tomb
yet I dread
the jolt
that takes
us further
nearer
what

Exile is easier now.
An hour in a car queue,
two hours bounced
in a tin-plate catamaran,
a day-trip to a new life.

CHAPTER 14

Among lettered folk

I

I should have guessed.
The woman behind the library desk looked mournful
when I asked about transcription services.

'There are no short cuts to scholarship,'
she intoned, adjusting her specs,
'You must transcribe each letter word by word,
after a while you'll recognise the writing,
words will come easier.
Have you discussed this with our archivist?'

I shook my head regretfully –
sorrow seemed the only response
for my scholarly inadequacies.

She sighed. "Go out of here, turn left
and the furthest door is archives.
You'll have to make an appointment.'

The girl at the Archives desk
was friendlier, enthusiastic,
eyeing my jiffy bag like it was riches.

"We've lots of material that could help.
Did you know that many Welsh went out there too,
chasing the gold they found in the early 50s?
There was even a famous shipwreck
here in Anglesey, the Royal Charter,
it was said to be carrying Australian gold."

That rang a bell. I'd seen a memorial somewhere.
And one of the letters had mentioned goldfields –
we scholars just love synchronicity!

II

Extract from Fiona Sheehan's journal
18th February 2003

Out to dinner with staff from the uni.
We speak of linguistics and belles lettres,
the more letters, the better in this game.

We range from etymology
of testaments and testifying,
to vegetable pigments mutandis –
root crops that were too lingam-like
in their state of grace – to Celts, to languages
that live and die and half-live on sign-posts.

A request to pass the salt
stops conversation mid-thrust.
A puzzled, embarrassed look
at what 'salth' might be,
or indeed whath 'mighth' might be
for those who thought
a soft Irish t
was just the breakfast
variety.

The crispness of exchange,
tight, precise, now stalled
by the lingering, moist
half-sibilance of another culture,
of another rooth crop
mutating in full view.

III

After a slow start
I began to make good progress,
went into Bangor most days,
exchanged small talk
with the girl behind the desk, got
an occasional smile out of the archivist.

The second week in, I decided
to take a break from the letters, was immersed
in an 1849 almanac for Australian emigrants
when the door opened. I glanced up,
caught a pale blue eye in the tanned face
of a man, mid-30s I guessed, stringy, lean,
looking a little choked in his shirt and tie.

Not that my antennae were immediately raised
but he was younger than anyone I'd met already
and might be worth a coffee.
Didn't think he was from round here, the tan suggested
he'd be happier out of doors than in dusty archives.

He gave a quick, shy jerk of facial muscles
before sitting down, opposite,
opening a lever-arched file, waiting while
the assistant brought him his reading matter,
then getting down to work, head down.
It was clear I'd have to make the running here.

IV

Lancaster of Liverpool, Gilks, Master, burthen 748 Tons, from the Port of Liverpool to Sydney, New South Wales, the 12th September 1854

Surname	Given name	Station	Age	Of what nation	Status	Comments
Gilks	William	Captain	43	British	Crew	
Nicklennight	Daniel	Mate	23	British	Crew	
Donaldson	Joseph	Carpenter	23	British	Crew	
Bissett	William	Carps Mate	24	British	Crew	
Perry	Walter	Boatswain	25	British	Crew	
Bridges	Robert	Sailmaker	58	British	Crew	
?	Cornelius	Steward	25	British	Crew	
Wee ?	John	Cook	34	British	Crew	
?	Andrew	Seaman	23	British	Crew	
Garn ?	John	Seaman	22	British	Crew	
Kelly	Michael	Seaman	32	British	Crew	
Thompson	William	Seaman	38	British	Crew	
Adangton	William	Seaman	21	British	Crew	
Langley	William	Seaman	21	British	Crew	
Quin	Chares	Seaman	24	British	Crew	
Scott		O.S.	19	British	Crew	
Hitchcock	Edward	O.S.	20	British	Crew	
Price	James	O.S.	24	British	Crew	
White	Andrew	O.S.	40	British	Crew	
Paterson		Seaman	24	British	Crew	
Hughes	George	2nd Steward	18	British	Crew	
Henderson	William	Joiner	24	British	Crew	
Roberts		Seaman	29	Trieste	Crew	
Xanstrie		Seaman	27	Trieste	Crew	
Canstrick		Seaman	21	Trieste	Crew	
Arles		Seaman	22	Boston	Crew	
Dawson	John	Apprentice			Crew	
Robins		Apprentice			Crew	

Surname	Given name	Station	Age	Of what nation	Status	Comments
James	Thomas R.				Passenger	
James	Sarah				Passenger	
Fairhurst	Mary				Passenger	
Hogg	James				Passenger	
Reed	Geo.				Passenger	
Reed	Ann				Passenger	
Reed	Henry				Passenger	
Martin	Sarah				Passenger	
Brady	Edward				Passenger	
Patterson	Robert				Passenger	
Webster	Geo.				Passenger	
Johnstone	John N.				Passenger	
Butler	William				Passenger	
Butler	Joseph				Passenger	
Butler	Michl.				Passenger	
Butler	Thos				Passenger	
Butler	Margt.				Passenger	
Butler	Mary				Passenger	
Butler	Bridget				Passenger	
Butler	Catherine				Passenger	
Butler	Patrick				Passenger	
Waddell	John				Passenger	
Waddell	Ann				Passenger	
Waddell	John				Passenger	
Waddell	George				Passenger	
Waddell	Robert				Passenger	
Waddell	James				Passenger	
Waddell	Thomas				Passenger	
Humphreys	Geo.				Passenger	
Cleaton	Wm.				Passenger	
Gray	Robert				Passenger	
Gray	Elizabeth				Passenger	
Rogers	Mary				Passenger	
Rogers	Elizabeth				Passenger	

Surname	Given name	Station	Age	Of what nation	Status	Comments
Rogers	Robert				Passenger	
Creagh	Robert				Passenger	
Lester	Thomas				Passenger	
James	Thomas R.				Passenger	
James	Sarah				Passenger	
Lester	Elizabeth				Passenger	
Lester	John				Passenger	
McDonald	Bridget				Passenger	
McDonald	Rosehama				Passenger	
McDonald	John				Passenger	
McDonald	Michl.				Passenger	
McDonald	George				Passenger	

V

Amazing what you can find
on the Net these days.

This particular catch
hauled in an entire list
of names, ages, nationalities,
for the Lancaster's voyage.

Blanks where the captain's hand shook
and the transcriber wouldn't hazard a guess,
or put a question mark where she could.

I scanned the rows
of mates and ordinary seamen,
mere boys, some of them,
although four months at sea
would have made men of them,
aged them in brine.

We weren't told how old
the passengers were, though most
seemed in family groups, or couples.

Here and there a single name,
some men and a woman; did any unite
their fortunes by the end of the voyage?

The largest group were the Butlers,
nine of them crowning the list
as they probably did the dinner table.

All present and accounted for, save Edward,
though I'd guess the Captain erred
and called him Patrick, the default for Irishman.

VI

The guy from the archives is giving a talk tonight.
I saw the poster on the notice-board:
'Fatal shore – 19th century emigrants in Australia'
by Dr Michael Jenkins, a string of letters following.
It will make a change from lectures
on Welsh bards or triple-harpists.

I could even get to have a proper talk with him,
show off my new-found erudition about the Antipodes
(eg, his title comes from Robert Hughes).

In the Archives, we've barely said hello,
but there are moments when I catch his eye
and he actually blushes! Which may be a sign
of interest, though most men I knew
wouldn't be caught dead
admitting interest.

More fool me. I'd think it was an act,
the sustained wriggle
of the salmon on the line.

Wrong every time.
He'd turn out to be the fisherman
who'd throw his catch back.

VII

The lecture had gone well.
Dr Jenkins proved a decent speaker
after a few painful bouts of throat-clearing.

It seems he's descended from some old cove
who left Wales in the 1860s
to make his fortune in Australia.
Joseph Jenkins didn't seem to mind leaving
a wife and a brace of children behind
or a farm he hadn't managed to drink away.

But he brought the most important things:
his mother tongue, a diary that he wrote up
religiously and a Welsh Bible that kept him alive
during 20 years in New South Wales
living the swagman's life,
bemoaning his fate till he came home again.

When he forgot himself, Mike Jenkins
was engaging in a tweedy sort of way.
Having nothing better on,
I waited for the crowds to disappear
before making my approach
to suggest comparing notes over tea.

Chapter 15

Wild Colonial Girl

Yass, New South Wales
12th April 1852

It's a small town, a scatter
of huts and sheds at the edge of bush
where the sheepmen come once a week
to buy or trade stock, to get provisions,
to drink what they've sold.

I work in the grocery store.
The boss is a Norfolk man
who said right off he thought the Irish
lower than the low.
To prove his point he put me straight
to cleaning out the privy,

I wasn't allowed to serve
until I'd proved to him I wouldn't run off
with his foodstock.
But at least he feeds me regular;
I've heard stories of other girls
near starved to death.

So I'll bide my time,
keep an eye out
for a new situation,
sweet talk the sheepmen
who come in.

Meanwhile the nights are mine.
I can walk out among the trees,

watch the sky, the spread of stars
in shapes I don't yet recognise.

And sounds I never dreamed of:
wild dogs calling to each other,
the screech of birds
they call kookaburras.

Yass
19th December 1853

Here, you are
what you make yourself.
There's a man who sweeps the street
and sleeps in a battered shed
on the outskirts of town.

He speaks to nobody,
no-one to him,
though he is a common sight
in town, dragging his brush
up and down the streets.

The children have their fun
in plaguing him.
They run up to his door –
that is, the planks of wood
he's laid against the entrance –
and throw stones until the din
raises him from slumber.

Once they set fire to the corner
of the shed and sat and laughed
while he raised a dust storm
quenching it.

He's Welsh, a temperance man
who they say was once
a prosperous farmer,
though you'd never know
to look at him,
sad wreck of a man.

He tried his luck
down at the diggings in Victoria,
even struck gold once or twice

but lost it all to mates
who were less lucky, more devious.

He says he'll return home one day,
meantime he stays, writes
in his battered old book,
poems, he says, and jottings,
and remembers
what the bible said
about Ruth and the alien corn.

Sydney
15th October 1856

Fr Maginnis was as good as his word.
He promised he would find me a job
if I returned from Goulbourn.
So I came back, weary of heart, sad
to leave so many friends at the station.

But I could see it wasn't wise to stay
once the Missis had taken against me.
She was alright at first, seemed glad
to have someone from home to talk to.
We had many good chats out on the veranda
after the little ones were bathed and sleeping.

Then the Master broke his leg and was round the house
and under our feet though he seemed a good laugh
and was always joking, sure there was no harm in him.
So I didn't see at first the Missis' face darkening
or I would have recognised that pinched look,
the sharp glance meant trouble.

When Father came to say his monthly Mass
she must have had a word
because he took me aside
and asked me would I leave with him.
He's a kind man, he doesn't judge,
unlike many of his sort.
His God makes time for sinners,
though I'm not one.

The new position is at a place near Berrima
in the Southern Highlands
with a family who came out in '54.
Butlers from Kilkenny –
well got from what he tells me –
one is headed for a judge,

others are grazing sheep
in the thousands.

The best thing is there is no Missis;
the place is run by a spinster sister
who finds it all too much –
I'll soon tame her.

Chapter 16

At home at Woodlands

Woodlands, Australia
31st March 1855

Dearest Forristal

This is by way of sending you our new address as we have finally secured the lease and moved here in February. The process was a lengthy one – Edward was forced to go from pillar to post in the Governor's office in an attempt to sort the matter out. But in the end things were settled to everyone's satisfaction and we have our new home.

I must confess my heart sank when I first saw the dwelling. It is very small, not being one half of the dimensions of Pleaberstown, having just six bedrooms, a dining room, parlour and kitchen. It is also of a wooden construction that seems very frail and vulnerable to the wild winds they have here. But Edward was assured that this was the most suitable material for the climate (cool in summer, cosy in winter) and he has great plans to add more rooms and turn it into a homestead fit for the Butlers. Michael approved of the grazing land (we've 200 acres) and the boys were delighted with the wild prospect of the hills that surround us. We are hopeful that Father will join us soon.

I plan to have a small kitchen garden where I can grow vegetables and I am told that fruit does very well here, so an orchard will follow. In truth there is so much work to be done that I despair of ever completing it, and all the time my heart hearkens back to the familiar fields around our old home, and the friendly warmth of Ballyogan. But there is no choice but to persevere, and pray. For God must find his way to so distant a place.

I will end here, cousin, before the tears fall too plentifully. I know it upsets my sisters and brothers and I will appear cheerful for their sake. Fondest regards to all,

your cousin, Margaret Butler

Woodlands, Australia
1st November 1856

My ever dearest Forristal, Aunt Bessy, Uncle Martin and cousins

I trust this letter finds you all well. Please forgive the delay in responding to your last most welcome letter. To tell the truth, I have been feeling in low spirits for the past few months with my old ailment and it has been such a struggle to keep this household going. Woodlands is no Pleaberstown – dust gets everywhere; I have only to sweep out a room when a storm rises and fills the place again. And what an effort to grow the vegetables we eat at table, none which look like the ones we grew at home.

My brothers and sisters are well but, much as I love them, it is such hard work feeding and cleaning for them, especially since Eliza left last Spring. We have had word from her last month. She is settling in well at Ipswich, the Sisters are kind and she is looking forward to taking her vows next Easter. I envy her the contentment she has found.

Edward came to visit in August. He is now well established in his legal career and has built a fine new home for him and Sarah at Darling Point, where the best families in Sydney live. He got the notion whilst here that I needed help so had a word with Bishop Clohessy when he got back with the result that we have a new member of the household now, a young Limerick girl, a Murphy from Bruree, who came over on the workhouse orphans scheme some years back.

Lizzie is a mean-looking thing; she stares at you straight in the eye and won't look down for anything. She keeps the place clean but only because I'm always watching her – you can sure that quick as whip she'd be up to mischief if let. And she's quite affected – she already has that nasty twang that the squatters' wives have here. She's good with the younger ones though. She can turn her hand to most anything.

Joseph seems more settled these days. He was very restless some months back and seemed about to leave – the papers are full of all those gold-strikes and he's determined to make his fortune with a claim. He's still only 15. He's much too young to venture off on his own. This is such a dangerous country but I don't know how much longer I can protect him. Edward says I worry too much, and perhaps I do.

So tell me all your news, cousin dear. How fare all the children? Are they still all at home? What of little John, my sweet little Duck-Man. Does he remember his old aunt now so far away? What news from the parish? And how fares Pleaberstown? I cannot tell you how often I think about that dear place, and home. Sometimes I fancy that in my mind's eye I can recreate the town, the houses, the little bridge, the protestant church, the smallest detail, that if I stare long enough at the sky once the sun has set I might catch a glimpse of something familiar. Then I blink and see the same blank sky, the same scattering of unrecognisable stars. How I do go on! Please write soon, and be a better correspondent than your cousin, Margaret B.

CHAPTER 17

Extract from Fiona Sheehan's journal 20th February 2003

Margaret 10

Who named it
Woodlands
The few trees
seem parched
their bark
like paper
coming off
in strips
roots are
bare knuckles
clawing into
baked earth

Margaret 11

Edward took the post
to Berrima
the first chance
to let F know
to name the place
we have
washed up in
E returned
said it would take
six months
for a response
like dropping

Shall I expand the cast list?

Margaret at odds with Lizzie right away, snobbery, or does she sense like a mother hen … Lizzie the fox?

What might L sound like, I wonder?

Still no form … Margaret doesn't seem to want it …

stones down
a well
never hearing
the splash

Margaret 12

There is a forest
a ten-mile ride
there and back
the first place
I forget
I am not home
old trees
green canopy
that hides
the strange sun
flies bite
familiarly
leaves crunch
dissolve
in dust
I could be
by Ballyogan's
oaks again
if I stop my ears
ignore the laugh
of galah birds

Margaret 13

I will not
show
I will not
bow
to her
straight back
her blue gaze
She will learn
to look down
when I
enter the room

Margaret 14

Eliza takes
her vows
a new name
hair shorn
black habit
shrouding her
gold ring
fastens her
to God
My finger
bare
age swells
knuckles
plumps the skin
where
the band
would have
lain.

Chapter 18

Walking out

I

Extract from Fiona Sheehan's journal
22nd February 2003

My hands are my best feature,
neat, too small to span
the full scale on the piano
and when I let the nails grow,
remember to file and shape
they're quite presentable.

I go ringless usually
and so forget the empty space,
the full tan, bare skin,
the tell-tale lack of gold
tagging me like some rare
migrant that's just flown in.

But others see, glance automatic,
smiles smug as they add me
to their latest endangered list.

II

I woke slowly, my head clogged,
sodden with too much wine and the sense
that something had happened too soon.

Ungluing my eyes, I shot a glance
to the other side of bed;
at least I'd had the wit
to send him home,

I couldn't face a breakfast of small talk
and false intimacies, the pretence
that a night of tangled limbs meant ever afters.

Details came trickling back.
His shy grin as if he'd just discovered
Van Diemans Land in the cleft of my breasts,
the way he called me *cariad*, as if
he chose his superlatives carefully
and meant this one. Way too soon for that.

My stomach lurched, I needed
a cup of tea to keep the panic down.
I stripped the bed while waiting for the kettle's hum.

III

Mike texted me. Seems we'd made a date
for morning coffee in the flea-pit
they call the refectory at the uni.

He really isn't my type, too easy to read.
Perhaps this offered a chance
to end it quickly.

So I was there prompt, clean,
a dash of lippy keeping
the self-loathing subliminal.

At ten past he dashed in, blurting apologies.
In his old man's tweeds
he didn't look like a life changer.

As he played with his filofax my breathing slowed,
the needle pricks in each temple eased.
I agreed, dinner might be nice, his place, Friday.

IV

Extract from Fiona Sheehan's journal
25th February 2003

Hours of seeking the path,
taking wrong turns at stiles
and kissing gates,
mis-reading maps,
following arrows round bends,
dead-ends or boggy steps.

Then rain began,
a soft cue that shelter
lay beneath pine-trees,
in the hush of scattered drops;
that a fallen trunk would bolster us
for as long as it took.

Chapter 19

Serving the Butlers

Woodlands
6th December 1856

I've been here two months
and already know
whose bread to butter,
when to keep quiet,
when to chat.

Fr Magennis came with me from Sydney
to pay my fare and see me 'settled in'.
He speaks highly of Master Edward,
mentions good connections
and the need to please my Mistress at all times.

That would be the oldest girl, Margaret.
She has the face of soured cream -
and she wanders around the house in a dream
as if she's lost something valuable.
Nothing pleases her –
the weather is hot, the food mean.

Nothing is like home.

Nor should it be.
I would have thought she'd be glad
to shake the earth off of that miserable place.

A more pampered bunch I never saw,
faces scrubbed, plump arms, hands soft,
nobody to look crossways at them.

Kate, the youngest girl, is a quieter type.
She's gentle and kind to me;
she helps out in the kitchen, has a way
of brightening even Margaret up.
She spends much of the day in her room,
quiet at prayer.

The boys are grand.
They behave when Edward is there,
but when he has left for Sydney
they are as boisterous
as they ought to be.
There's plenty of land
to keep them occupied
and Michael has built up a large flock.

But all the young ones can speak of
is taking their chances on the gold fields.
They bury themselves in accounts of sudden riches.
Even young Joseph, though I'm sure
Miss Margaret would not let him go.
She watches over him
like a broody bantam.

Woodlands,
31st December 1856

A new addition to the household.
Edward rode out from Sydney one Sunday
and brought with him an old,
worn man in shabby clothes.

He looked the type
that often turned up at the workhouse
and rarely lasted long,
hunger eating them up from the inside,
no strength to work,
sitting where they could find a spot.
He minded me of that old man in Yass.

But for all his jaded look
there was a likeness you couldn't miss
and there could be no mistaking
the way the sisters fussed around him,
taking off his shoes, sitting him down,
soothing him with cups of tea and soft words.

Miss Margaret came to the kitchen later.
She didn't explain much
(she likes to keep her secrets)
but said her father had newly arrived
and should be made as comfortable as possible.
She gave me a list of his favourite foods;
where she thought I'd find fresh salmon
I can't fathom.

He'd been a Steward for the road builders
but didn't look like he had worked
this long time, nor would he again.

When I brought supper up –
I found him and Joseph thick as thieves.

In the glow of the gas-light they looked
more like grandfather and grandson.

The old man kept asking Joe
to repeat himself but wouldn't admit
he was hard of hearing.
Mostly he just gazed into the fire,
ignoring the swirl of talk,
keeping his emigrant thoughts
to himself.

Woodlands 12th February 1857

Flummery, the old man's favourite.

Miss Margaret mixes flour and water
(no more than a tablespoon)
stirs well, her mouth thin,
knuckles white on the spoon
as if she thinks it might escape her.

She pours the paste
into a pan on the hearth,
stirs again until she sees bubbles
blistering the milky broth.

Then she adds gelatine
(a teaspoon, no more, no less
at the price McCormack charges)
and, lord help us, a whole cup of sugar.
Then four of our own oranges,
freshly squeezed, a lemon
and the pulp of passionfruit.

She stirs again,
then takes it off the heat
and pours it into a dish
resting on crushed ice.

She carries it out
like it was the crown jewels
and leaves it in the cold store,
12 hours and more
till it is set and ready
for his High Tea.

Not so much as a mutter out of him
as he keeps his head down
and cleans his plate,
sucks his spoon.
She watches every mouthful
with a mother's care.

Chapter 20

Extract from Fiona Sheehan's journal 26th February 2003

THREATENED SPECIES RECORDED WITHIN THE LOWER HUNTER CENTRAL COAST REGION

Note – Found this on the net … might be useful for local detail. Some lovely sounds

Bynoe's Wattle (*Acacia bynoeana*)
Coastal Spurge (*Chamaesyce psammogeton*)
White-flowed Cynanchum (*Cynanchum elegans*)
Tranquillity Mintbush (*Prostanthera askania*)
Charmhaven Apple (*Angophora inopina*)
Thick Lip Spider Orchid (*Caladenia tessellata*)
Heart-leaved Stringybark (*Eucalyptus camfieldii*)
Slaty Redgum (*Eucalyptus glaucina*)
Magenta Lilly Pilly (*Syzgium paniculatum*)
Green and Golden Bell Frog (*Litoria aurea*)
Regent Honeyeater (*Xanthomyza phrygia*)
Southern Brown Bandicoot (*Isoodon obesulus*)
Red-crowned Toadlet (*Pseudophryne australis*)
Wallum Froglet (*Crinia tinnula*)
Yellow-bellied Sheathtail Bat (*Saccolaimus flaviventris*)
Eastern Falsistrelle (*Falsistrellus tasmaniensis*)
Squirrel Glider (*Petaurus norfolcensis*)
Spotted-tail Quoll (*Dasyurus maculatus*)
Brush-tailed Phascogale (*Phascolgale tapoatafa*)
Long-nosed Potoroo (*Potorous tridactylus*)
Sanderling (*Calidris alba*)
Painted Snipe (*Rostratula benghalensis*)
Comb-crested Jacana (*Irediparra gallinacea*)
Turquoise Parrot (*Neophema pulchella*)
Powerful Owl (*Ninox strenua*)
Grey-crowned Babbler (*Pomatostomus temporalis*)

Margaret 15

This is a place
of ghosts
heat
blanches skin
then turns it
into leather
like the thing
I saw once
taken from
the bog
near
Pleaberstown
trees
calcify
become
skeletons
their silver
limbs
dazzle
till I look
into the sun

Margaret 16

My father
went away
his grandfather
has returned
in his place

Margaret 17

Each night I am
the last thing
that he sees
I plump his pillow
settle sheets
rub his heels
with balsam
made from herbs
and goats milk
he says it soothes
to have me
say his prayers
for him
to have me
kneel for him
before his God.

Extract from Fiona Sheehan's journal 27th March 2003

I

This morning, my darling, as the sun came up
and the mountains stretched their curves out
and the sea was a great rippling mirror for yachts

the swifts filled the sky, swooping,
settling just a second, round an old nest
collapsed for weeks beneath a window sill.

They darted and dived and perched a while
before resuming their deep arcs,
a blurring of sleek lines back and forth

as if they had finally realised
they had over-stayed and must imprint
the smell, the feel, of that tattered hive,

the way I keep returning to your lips,
not believing that this could be memory,
that I'll wake up some day on the other side.

II

We both read maps
as poorly
as we read ourselves,
not knowing yet
the ordnance of a back,
the topography of an inner arm.

We reached the highest point at Moelfre
when the sun was edging round
from South Stack, casting shadow

on the memorial stone, a demure slab
detailing the night when 400 souls
were lost to waves and rocks.

October hurricanes reminded villagers
crowding the cliff's edge that the sea
was no respecter of Australian gold.

Or did it covet it?
Shingle is yellow here, a fleeting sparkle
amid the Methodist grey of Anglesey.
The gold lures divers still,
dreamers
of every kind.

We prospected the ledge,
looking for tormentil,
found only yellow furze
to hold on to,
to give us purchase
against the glittering spray.

III

He brought roses.
Now, the first signs of wilt, silk
underpetals curling into themselves,
velvet interlaying tighter
to keep the light trapped
in the latticework of veins.

It's been 20 years since I first dreamt
that every girl's reward
came with red petals and green ferns.

So I'll preserve them with warm water
laced with a witch's brew

of sachet powder,
watch each morning
as the petals fall, one by one
and gather them up,
sealed with hot wax and vellum envelope
I've kept all these years
for that very purpose.

Extract from Fiona Sheehan's journal
28th March 2003

It comes more easily
when acts of love require
acts of taking leave,

the coaxing in,
the easing out
of another's body.

So you are always prepared
for the latest leave-taking
to be the final one,

a moment to look back,
shut the door, assess
the chance of other openings.

CHAPTER 21

Bereavement

Woodlands, Australia
29th May 1857

Dear cousin Forristal

It is my sad duty to tell you that Father died here at Woodlands on 24th May, after succumbing to an illness bravely borne for many months. He had never fully recovered from the stroke that afflicted him more than two years ago, although we had hoped that he might last for some years yet, with our care. But it was not to be, God willed otherwise.

The first great change came over him in January, and he sank fast after that. We were not sure he would survive till Easter, and indeed he received the last sacraments from Father Maginnis (a Kilkenny man) on Good Friday, it was a solemn and touching scene. But then he rallied, although it was clear he never would again be the man he had been, we had hope again. Indeed he was little more than a living skeleton, and spent his days praying and preparing for death. His death was truly edifying – he accepted God's will with great patience and tranquillity, a lesson to us all. He died peacefully in the bosom of his family – only distance kept Eliza and Edward from being there. God Rest His Soul.

I will conclude with other news. We are all in reasonable health. Edward thrives – he now has the position of Crown Prosecutor for the District Court in Sydney, while his legal business brings in £500 a year. His wife, Sarah, is tall and dashing-looking. They have no children yet. Here at

Woodlands we have been making some improvements and now have two good rooms for parlour and drawing room, eight sizeable bedrooms, a storeroom and a kitchen with oven. The latter is Lizzie's demesne, and one does not bother her there. She has notions, that girl, but I have learned that it is easiest to keep out of her way.

You may have seen an account in the papers of the new gold fields they've found. They call them the 'Snowy River' diggings and they are making the fortune of many. It is only 100 miles from us so three of the boys intend to go out in the Spring and to try their luck. Joseph intends to go and there's no holding him, no matter what I say. I pray that St Christopher will watch over him, though I fear that it is more a matter for St Jude's good offices!

Please give my love to Bessy and the little ones and tell Billy Butler that we received his letter a few days after Father's death. I will reply shortly.

William, Joe, Mike, Thomas and the girls unite with me in fondest feelings of love and affection to you and all enquiring friends.

Your cousin, Margaret Butler

Woodlands,
3rd June 1857

The old man has gone and it is a mercy.
The last few weeks there was nowhere to go
in this house without hearing his breaths,
hoarse and laborious, stopping and starting.

At first we had no rest,
waiting to see if each pause
had sent him to his Maker,
then it would start up again
the rasp and wheeze of
something grasping at life.

In the end we got used to it,
learned to wait,
barely lifted our heads
when the house quietened,
only knew he was dead
when the pause lengthened.
and the sobs began.

Margaret gave instructions.
I was to lay him out, wash the body
then cook a fine meal for the Bishop
who'd given him the last rites,
a fine feast to befit the priest
of this last Irish chieftain.

Some chieftain.
Little more than
bleached bones
washed up on the shore.

Chapter 22

Extract from Fiona Sheehan's journal
1st April 2003

Three years ago today the phone rang.
I picked it up expecting a plan
for pints, some salesman or other
and got instead dead air,
a pause full of static
then my mother's flat voice.

Dad had collapsed.
I could hear words
like hospital, surgery,
but the sounds didn't seem in order.
I couldn't control the spasm in my throat,
my lungs filling, the receiver falling.

Nine days we spent in the waiting room.
We came, we went, put money in the meter,
read papers, did crosswords
but mostly we just sat and stared
at the one picture on the wall,
something by Constable, I remember.

Dad pulled a Lazarus.
Doctors preened their bright whites,
spoke of Lancet write-ups,
then looked grave and told us
what we could expect of a man
of his age when he came home,
which he did eventually.

The routine resumed,
the panic subsided.
I did my fair share
for the first few months,
then the visits grew rarer.

I was busy, didn't have time
to run that errand, fetch the paper.
In truth, I couldn't face my spectre father.

Margaret 18

No struggle
at the end
not peace
not acceptance
of God's will
just a slipping away
a slowing of breath
so gradual
we hardly felt
it stop
what was left
a husk
a breeze
would have
scattered

Margaret 19

I am too old
for an orphan
there is no one
to look above to
none beneath
to nurture
Joe will fly soon
he already
puffs up
his feathers
when that girl
looks his way

Chapter 23

Losses and Gains

Woodlands 31st December, 1858

He is nine years younger than me.

Each evening he walks me out,
shows me the run of the farm,
the way the land curves with the creek,
stretches so far you have to squint
to see the boundary.

He describes what snakes to watch for,
warns of huntsmen,
forgets I've been here longer than him,
that I have already learned
the sun's arc is opposite to home.

He takes my hand,
identifies all the trees
that shade the farm house,
the spindly stringy-bark,
the wattle, the river gum,
the pungent eucalyptus.

He names the birds.
I know the collared doves,
plump on a bench, necks entwined,
and can recognise the red-backed wren
who darts like his Irish cousin

but he silences me
when he points out galah-birds,

the rosellas and lorikeets,
the blue-faced honeyeaters,
blacked-headed perdalots.

I watch his lips frame the words
as the dusk grows
and he continues his list
of plants and flowers.
He picks some yellow everlastings
as he walks me home.

Cambalong,
Snowy River
2nd February 1859

Dear Cousin Forristal

I trust this letter finds you in good health. You will be surprised to hear from me, I'm sure. Ed. and Mags are the letter writers in our family but I thought you would find a report on our hunt for gold to be of interest and that Bessy and the boys might like to know what life is like on the diggings. I've heard the papers over there are full of news about all that gold and there may be some tempted to try out for a prospector.

Tell them not to bother.

Joe and me have been here six months and for all the nuggets we've seen, we might as well have stayed with Mike and his sheep up at Woodlands. We quickly got a claim for £2, bought our tent and materials and spent our days crouching by the river's flow, sieving and sifting.

Life is hard. A man can break his back 12 hours a day, digging in mud, drenched in water, and still find nothing more than flakes of pyrite (they call it *fool's gold* – no lack of *amadawns* here). And Joe and I are young – there are men here better than 60 years of age digging and picking for scraps.

The only ones who make a buck are the shoe-makers. It seems every last man must have his boots imported and the price you give for a pair of Wellington boots shipped from England is £1. Tea and coffee is half a guinea a pound and soap cannot be found at all in the diggings – in all the dirt we all end up looking the same, the Irish, the blacks and yellow Chinamen who dig here. Mind you, many of the Celestials, as they call them here, are coining it anyway. They grow vegetables and sell on to the diggers at a profit. Some have even opened up small shacks to sell the quare food of theirs – not a spud in sight.

We do not intend to stay much longer here. The companies have bought up most of the claims along the River, we'll not make money here. Joe seems anxious to get back and there are reports of new finds up in Mudgee, which is closer to home. So we'll not be sending any fortune back to Ireland.

I'm writing this by candlelight and at 3s a wick they're precious things, so I'll stop now. Give all our love to Bessie and the boys,

your cousin, William Butler

Woodlands
1st April, 1859

Back home
the earth betrayed them,
rich clay pulpy
with purple mush,
new growth gone bad.

Blight, they called it,
rot, God's judgement
on their lazy-beds,

one year, the next,
the next,
until hope lay
unburied
with old stalks,

another bad smell
among heaps of waste
littering the roadside.

Here, forgetting,
they buy new spades,
take up tools they never
thought they'd use again
in new earth, new stone,

break hard ground,
sifting the fill,
holding their breath
for the tell-tale glint
that divides the hungry
from the full.

Woodlands
3rd April 1859

The letter came today.
Miss Margaret was so relieved
she read it to me,
came into the kitchen and sat by me,
not guessing how keen I was
to hear the news.

I'd only agreed that Joe should go
when he promised
the first nugget he found
would make a wedding ring.
He took a piece of string with him
sized from my finger
so he'd get the measure right.

Of course he had a different tale
for Margaret.
It has been a trial
since he's been gone.
He was her darling,
took her mind off
her own troubles,
stopped her harping on
about home and Ireland.

Now, six months on,
there's no sign of rings or riches.

The boys work 12 hours a day digging
and sifting by the water's edge,
finding nothing but fools gold
and blisters and bad backs.

The boys don't plan to stay;
Joe will come back,

Bill intends take a berth
with the next gold shipment to Liverpool.
If he can't find his own gold
he might as well take money
for those who'd better luck.

Joseph has stretched his wings.
Perhaps he'll come back
and not notice
when those wings are clipped.

CHAPTER 24

Moving in, moving on

I

Mike thinks my place is too small.
He has a pained look,
each time he comes over,
says the walls are closing in
that he's crowded out by piles of books,
by houseplants dotting the bay window,
which leaks, naturally.
How can I stand to live
in such cramped conditions?

He says the next step
is to find a place together.
He has a field trip lined up
but once he's back
and he's renewed his contract
with the Department
we should think about
taking things a little further.

So he's started to pore
over property supplements,
makes lists, ticks off the pros and cons
of various locations.

He hasn't noticed yet
that I always change the subject,
that I like my leaky bay,
that books pile up where
I want them,

that I never signed up
for a permanent fixture.

II

Extract from Fiona Sheehan's journal
21st April 2003

i

It could have gone either way
but the stroked cheek, the gentle caress
on this post-prandial sofa
ends in breaths slowing into sleep
as your body sags, zig-zags into my contours,
your head rests on my shoulder.

I stroke, fingers finding their pace,
not knowing the name for the tingle
in my throat, or the way my heart
struggles between beats, now soft, now fierce.

I keep a look out for predators,
unsure if my own thoughts won't feed
on your exposed skin,
the three-veined throb
at your temple.

ii

The year turns. A raincoat drips
off the back of the chair
you sat in to catch the changing light.

You could sit for hours
when things were fresh
and heart-stopping.

When we last met,
you sat by me, head-achy,
my head exploding with counter-arguments.

I looked across, searching for what caught me,
seeing instead an assortment of nose, eyes, ears, lips
that I ought to love.

Where does it go, then,
that perfect vision,
that only-you certainty?

Leaving instead (Picasso-style) –
an arrangement
of body parts.

iii

Forever on the chase
of a glorious sunset,
a happy ending,
we watch the dull disc
sink to the Irish Sea
behind a bank of cloud
that hasn't shifted all day.
Stubbornly hanging on like
a blind stuck on its cord,
leaving a gap wide enough
for a narrow chink
to ruddy the lighthouse.

The sea its habitual grey,
buff wavelets stiffening
in grumpy valediction,
pointing the way down
as if the sun needed
its daily reminder.

We await the finale,
the flashy striated pinks,
the last glint of light
when shapes appear
on the distant horizon,

a silhouette of curves,
of hills, of cliff faces,
aerial masts positioned
where I know I left them,
the familiar shape
of the bay, roofs, for god's sake
a church steeple.

In the instant it takes
to gasp my recognition
it's gone,
this Brigadoon stroke Dublin
and I'm left staring across
at a blank, sullen screen.

III

I needed good advice.
Who better to give it than Roisin,
veteran of romantic battlefields?

Though it had been a while
since we'd spent much time together
she knew me well,
how I ticked,
or didn't when it came to
clocks of a biological nature.

At Christmas we'd torn strips
off every type of man
we'd ever been with.
She'd recognise Mike's type,
be able to gauge from my description
whether this was one to keep
or if he was destined
to go the way of all flesh
I'd ever tangled with.

Her reply was swift;
she must sit up half the night
at her computer.

Her words were terse:
ditch him, cut loose,
why pay the price
for one man's neediness?

All they ever want is a substitute
for their mammy, except in the bedroom
and even that point was moot.

Once they have you where they want you,
looking up recipes, washing socks,

imagining nothing nicer than a quiet night in
then they bugger off, on to
the next sap who'd buy the fiction
that this one had a happy ending.

Reading between the lines I saw
that Roisin's latest must have done a bunk,
but that didn't make her wrong.

IV

What an eejit! I had the chance
last night, at coffee stage,
just before clearing up
the crumbs and spilt milk.
I'd casually dropped the fact
that I was staying put.

I didn't yet know my plans,
I'd more travel lined up,
couldn't commit
to setting up house with him.

For once Mike was direct.

"Is it over?"

I cleared my throat,
ready to pass judgement
but the pause grew
and my stupid tongue
locked.

Wasn't this
what I'd always wanted?
A decent man,
someone who put me first,
had good recipes for pasta?

I kicked for touch,
played for time:
we'd post-mortem it later.

V

Mike flew out to America.
I drove him to Manchester, car jammed
with luggage and unfinished arguments.

He still couldn't understand
why I wouldn't move in with him,
why I wanted to stay
with a pile of old papers
and a messy desk.

I didn't have the neck
to end it there at the airport,
in the crowds filing to check in,
Mike with his flustered,
where's my passport air,
his baffled smile, the sort of look
I'd last seen when we put the poodle down.
Trusting but in pain.

I'll see you when I get back.

Easier to let the tears come, then,
to turn away, to find the exit,
to rehearse all the way along the A55
the words I'd write to greet him
when he next logged on.

VI

Another email from Roisin.
She's heard from a long lost relation,
some contact of her auntie's.

She's based in New South Wales,
had reared her kids,
discovered genealogy
and tracked down Roisin's aunt
through the internet.

They'd begun to exchange
nuggets of family history
then the trail went dead
– or rather the auntie did –
now she's keen to revive it.

Roisin wants me to email her,
give her all the gen
on the Butler cousins.
Which is fine for her.
Fact is, I'm not all that keen
to let go an exclusive.

Chapter 25

Births, marriages, deaths

Woodlands, Australia
2nd December, 1859

My dearest cousin,

Life has been nothing but a catalogue of misery since we came to this dreadful country. Father's death was hard but he was a good age and had at least prepared to meet his Maker. It grieves me to tell you now that last month came news that our poor dear William has been lost at sea. He drowned when the steamer the Royal Charter went down off Anglesey.

Perhaps you have read an account in the paper – 400 souls were lost in a hurricane. William only took a berth at the last minute; a mate from Snowy River was transporting gold and offered Bill a share and a free passage to Liverpool. Bill was glad of the chance, and planned to come back out early next year on the return voyage.

The first we knew was when Edward rode out from Sydney with the news. We could hardly believe it. Joe, who had seen Bill most recently, went to his room, and wouldn't eat for days. Not even Lizzie, who it seems is now his great friend, could persuade him. And the worst thing, cousin dear, is that we cannot find out if William's body was recovered. There have been reports of bodies washed up as far as Ireland but so disfigured by the violent seas that none would know them.

It breaks our heart to think that our poor William might lie unclaimed and without sight of Christian burial. It is a great thing to ask, I know, dear cousin, but we would be for ever in your debt if you could undertake the hazardous journey over to Holyhead and try to find any trace of our poor boy. I have had word that the local reverend, a Mr Roose Hughes, has kept a record of all those lost and buried many of the drowned at his little church. Perhaps he might assist.

My heart is quite broken, and my prayers go unanswered.

Respects to Bessy and the children,
Mgt. Butler

Woodlands
30th April, 1860

He would have been 26 today.
No trace was found,
not so much as a shoe washed up.

Fr Magennis said mass in the parlour,
we all knelt in prayer,
heads bowed, murmuring
as the priest intoned,
the room drenched
with the smell of incense.

Afterwards, we went out
to the paddock to plant a tree,
though we hadn't found
the sapling of Mountain Ash
Miss Margaret wanted,

forcing instead into
hard ground
the silvery bark
of a eucalyptus,
the ghost gum tree
that grows in these parts.

Extract from Fiona Sheehan's journal
5th May 2003

Taken from Church Record Book, Pentraeth Church, Anglesey

11:11:1859. Female person.
Female person.
Female person.
14:11:1859. Male person.
15.11.1859. Male person.
1:12:1859. Male person.

Inscription on a memorial stone, Llanallgo Church, Anglesey

This monument has been erected by public subscription to the memory of those who perished in the wreck of the "Royal Charter" off Moelfre on the coast of Anglesey on her passage from Australia to England, Wednesday, the 26th October, A.D. 1859.

There Lie in this Churchyard the remains of 140 of the sufferers and 45 in the Churchyard of Penrhos Lligwy, all of whom were buried by the Pious and Charitable incumbent the Revd. Stephen Roose Hughes and his brother the Revd. Hugh Robert Hughes.

So many washed up unclaimed. Does he lie here in the rich red clay of a Welsh island?

Margaret 20

No sleep
for weeks.
How can I
till I know
he rests
has found
peace
with Father
I thought
danger
lay here
with snakes
poison bark
hot rain
hard clay
How could
I guess
he'd meet
death
in sight
of home.

Woodlands
2nd March 1863

I'm back at Loughrea,
stretched on my old cot,
the other beds empty,
the room dark but for
shafts of moonlight
that catch the motes
hanging in the air

and I'm shifting in bed;
I cannot find a way
to ease my limbs
out of hard angles
on this mattress
of straw and air.

The sounds begin
from the other side of the wall,
the softest murmur
of higher and lower tones
blending into each other.

And I can't guess
whose secret sweetness
I am listening to
but the cold grows around me
and the blanket slips
no matter what I do to grasp it.
I cannot move
to block my ears,
to let my breathing
drown it out.

Goulbourn,
15th June 1863

Fr Magennis arranged it.
At first he wouldn't help,
did not wish to risk the Butler ire
lest he see a dip
in his weekly collection.

But when he saw
the way it was with me,
how far gone, he must have thought
the arrival of a Butler bastard
a worse disaster.

So we slipped out
when Margaret went to town
and rode the 20 miles
in the early morning,
a June bride
braving the winter mists.

The priest said the blessing
as quickly as he could,
stumbling over the Latin.
We two stood, our third was
the priest's housekeeper
who kept shaking her head,
eyes closed, hands
grasped tight on a bone rosary
that clicked through her fingers.

We'll stay here a few days,
then ride back and face the wrath
of Mistress Margaret.
I wonder how she'll take
to her new sister.

Woodlands, Australia
2nd July 1863

My dearest Forristal

Please forgive my tardiness in replying to your so welcome letter of November last, which arrived here by the January Mail. Indeed, it offered great delight to us all, bringing as it did such precious visits from our cousins who we have not seen for so long. You can hardly imagine with what joy, and what astonishment each likeness was handed round the dinner table. We could barely trace resemblance to the little ones. Except for young Margaret, who retains the same good natured face we all recall so fondly.

But could that elegant young lady be little Ellen? Her portrait was immediately seized upon by her cousin Thomas who admired it so much he declared himself in love and placed her image by his in the family album. And what of young John? That dashing lad can hardly be my Duck Man, my rare pet with whom I spent such sweet days. Tears spring so readily to my eyes these days, I cannot see clearly to write.

I must say, however, cousin dear, I was a little disappointed in your own likenesses. Aunt Ansty would look better with her bonnet off and the artist did not do you justice for the handsome man you are. Do get them taken again, and add to them the likenesses of our dear friends Mrs Jones and Mr Baglins, so old acquaintances may be reunited again.

Edward says these new daguerreotypes are quite the rage in Sydney. He urges us all to sit for our portraits so we can send them home. I would rather not – from what I hear it is all explosions and bad smells and who would want to see this dried old maid? Australia's weather has not been kind to my complexion; I would prefer the soft rain of Pleaberstown on my face to the hot streams of Woodlands.

This Christmas, Thomas set out on a journey of 1,000 miles and paid his long promised visit here on St Stephen's Day – they call it Boxing Day, as they do in England, it's a godless place. His journey was eventful – he rode to Rockhampton, then travelled by steamer to Brisbane, called to see Bishop Quinn and then on to Ipswich to see our dear Eliza, who is in the convent there. En route his coach was stuck-up by bushrangers, who demanded cash from all who travelled there. Pity the poor Bank Clerk who had a bag crammed with notes. Tom had hidden some cheques in his boots so all he was parted with was a ten shilling note! He and Eliza laughed over the escapade when he was safely arrived in Ipswich. She is well and happy and is thriving in the tranquillity of God's service. I think she does better there than had she stayed at Woodlands.

The latest Butler baby, Edward's girl, is named Alice, for her mother's side. She was born on St Patrick's Day. And Joseph is married since June to Lizzie Murphy who has been with us since '56. I did not think it wise because her background is so very different (she was a Workhouse girl) but there was no talking to him and I could not prevail.

Pray forgive my blots and mistakes. Your cousin Margaret.

Woodlands, Australia
23 September, 1863

My ever dearest Forristal, Uncle Martin and Friends

All your letters dated June 20th arrived safely by the Sydney mail and must have crossed the one I sent in response to your earlier letter. I am glad to hear that you are doing well and news of your pleasant meetings and merry-making is a great pleasure to us all. It is as if we are there, in the drawing room at Ballyogan, seeing old friends and remembering happier times.

I can hardly believe that all my little cousins – both Forristals and Joyce – are now young gentlemen and maidens. I can only wish that their paths be smooth and bright and that they prove to be the pride and joy of their parents. I would also wish that some day they might meet their Australian cousins, but the Lord will decide such happenings.

My life passes in the same dull dull way. I get up early, pray, dust out my bedroom (although by half past three it's full of dust again!) and the dining room. I manage the dairy, sew, read a good deal though it is hard to find anything of interest, but mostly I think, my thoughts flying away to far off lands and far off times. I scarcely ever lie a night in bed without dreaming of that sea-beaten shore thousands of miles from here. But each morning I wake up in a foreign land.

My garden is my chief concern. I dig, I plant, I crop, I shade the young shoots from cold and sunshine but this country's harsh, ungenerous nature yields a scant, sickly return. I fancy the soil knows that I bear an Alien's heart towards it. Lizzie tries to help but she hasn't great strength these days.

These days I am quite the squatter. I now have three fat lambs as well as Eliza's tabby, Maggie. You will laugh when I say I love them all intensely but, in truth, I prefer these beasts to Australian mankind, or woman either.

I think I have now racked up all news of any interest. Forgive my little scraps of sentiment – remember how barren my life is and how limited my wanderings.

All unite with me, etc, Margaret

Chapter 26

Extract From Fiona Sheehan's journal
6th May 2003

Margaret 21

He was lost
so close
to shore
so close
to home
will the sea
yield him
to air
which side
will he
wash up

More poem possibilities.

Bad luck all round but Lizzie seems to find a way regardless. How would she sound?

And Margaret loses herself in duty.

Her making do frightens me.

Margaret 22

I found a feather
in the dust
russet rich
tiger striped
I picked it up
I could not say
which bird
one of many
that circle
blue sky
loop wide
their alien cries
I tucked it

into my belt
it lies snug
beneath
my alien heart

Margaret 23

Joe says
he is a man now
has no need
of a woman's care
though he's quick
to take her hand
I avoid
her smile
let her
sharp tone
merge with
screeching
birds
and bide
my time

CHAPTER 27

Family commitments

I

I decided to email Roisin's cousin.
A guilty thought that I was making capital
of some else's history
kept nagging me.

Besides, Flo could prove useful
for local information, might even know
if there were any scholarships going,
a grant, a nice bursary for
a visiting writer.

I woke up to her response
blinking on the mail-sweeper;
streuth she was keen.

She sent a very interesting attachment.
It seems she's a direct descendent of Lizzie B
and kept tabs on the rest of the tribe.
Best yet, she has her own pile
of ancient correspondence
from the Forristals of Ballyogan.

She asked if it mightn't
be a good idea to try
to bring the two sides together.

II

FAMILY TREE OF THE BUTLERS OF PLEABERSTOWN AND WOODLANDS

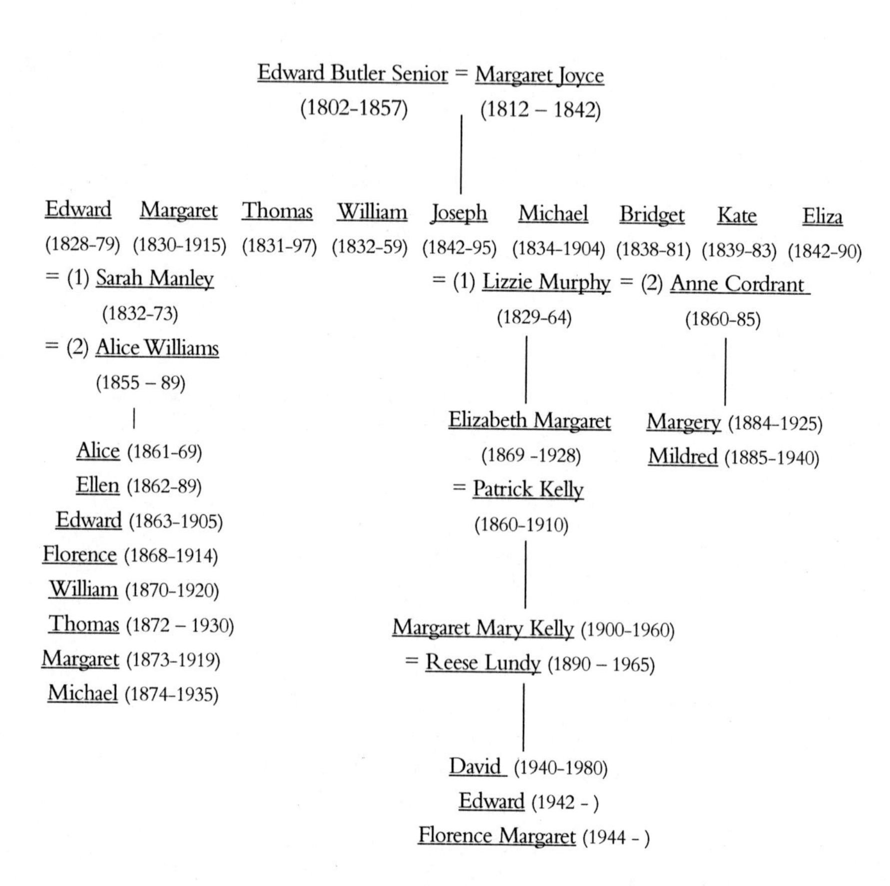

III

Genealogy required a quick trip home.

Mother made it clear
my presence was expected
at a gala night
to celebrate 40 years
of happy nuptials.

Births, marriages and deaths,
the only reason left
to get together.

IV

The photos come out. We gasp at their youthfulness,
try to guess what he was proclaiming
in his '40s tweeds and heart-throb hair-do,
admire her flawless skin, her Vermeer pearls.

Separate, then paired for dinner dances,
a rose in her hair, a corsage
he must have had help choosing.
Did her fingers tremble as she fastened his bow-tie?
Did they waltz to Mozart in the National Ballroom?

In one shot they seem to float in a garden corner,
old ivy creeping behind on a granite pillar
as she puts a flower in his button-hole.

Then the wedding day, her elegant in pink,
him laughing at the [best man?] photographer.
She hasn't learned, yet, that rictus grin
she'll use later as the kids arrive
and there's five of us urchin-like,
squat in the high grass, squinting at the lens.

She's grim custodian of the brave face,
consort for public occasions, bouffant neat
but the eyes focus on some distant spot
we can't imagine, the site of alternative
histories perhaps, a darkened room,
a quiet countryside, a frame empty of us.

V

Which is better?
The devil you know or
the angel who might bore you?

Chapter 28

Expectant

Woodlands, 12th October 1863

Cracked earth, dry ground,
grass burned off
into brown matting.
Lord knows when
the sky last darkened
and we felt His rain.

We get chores done by late dawn,
feed the hens, milk the cows
who can still yield.
Their throats are too dry
to low their distress,
they cough in their stalls.

Then we retreat,
find shade where we can,
it is enough
to feel sweat drip
from the base of our necks.

Margaret barely speaks.

Michael and Joe ride out.
Most days it is burial duty
though the ground is too hard,
so they gather the carcasses up,
pile them into pyres.

Smoke letters
on a blue sky.

The creek has run dry.
It trickles in the centre
of the hollowed bed,
jagged rocks dust-covered,
shrivelled curls of
water snakes.

I pray for the life
inside me, hope
it can still swim
its own current,
staunch its own tide.

Woodlands, 2nd December 1863

Nine months gone
and big as the new sow
Joseph brought back from Berrima.

We made a pen for her out back,
gathered straw and shavings
left behind from the fencing posts
made her snug as we could.

She doesn't move,
waiting for time or nature
or whatever will shift
the life inside her into cold air.

Mike says they'll be out by April,
could be up to eight bonamhs,
the start of a good herd.

Nobody names her.

Margaret wrinkles her nose,
talks of dirt, thinks up recipes for pork,
complains that we cannot grow
ingredients to go with it.

At night I sneak out,
lay a hand on her rough hide,
watch her bulk in the shade,
eyes tight and pink
behind thick lashes.

It's like she's dreaming
of a home she can't remember.

I've taken my skirts out
as far as they go,

next will be to sew panels in,
or else go about in shifts
like the natives do.

I wait, grow heavier,
feel my steps
go deeper in the earth,
trace the blue line
of the veins that lattice
my belly like marble,

let nature or time decide.

Extract from Fiona Sheehan's journal
16th May 2003

Three weeks late.
Each morning the trip,
the wait, the stomach lurch
at finding no red
dotting the towel,
clockwork abandoned.

The bathroom closes in,
wooden sauna
walls loom.

I take the kit out of the bag
crinkled from constant opening
and closing.

Nausea rises -
it could be a sign
or just nerves.

But I know what I don't want:
another life
has no claims on me.
It's too late for that;
I've watched friends, paid dues
with visits, teddies, the odd poem.

Not my time.
I put the box back, resolve
to wait a while longer.

Chapter 29

In two minds

I

Drought over,

so why
no smile
today?

II

Extract from Fiona Sheehan's journal
10th June 2003

Last night I dreamt of someone
not quite you. He had your features,
but the focus was blurred or else
you were a little thinner, a little shorter,
you stood on the earth a little differently,
this you, this not-quite-you.

This morning that memory has
evaporated like the moisture left by fog
on the deck as the sun breaks through.
I try to conjure you, your image near the surface
but obscured like the shape under leaves
of whatever forages beneath my bedroom window.

Perhaps the you, the not-quite-you
will resolve out of the dead air
of each trans-atlantic phone call,
out of the static-heavy pause
before your synthesised voice
answers a question I have not posed.

III

Off to London on a research trip.
There's a gale at Bangor station
and the landscape sways with the tilting train.

A child is crying down the carriage;
minutes later her red-faced mother
pushes her through feet-encumbered aisles.

Sweaty men in suits glare up from laptops,
fat women with shopping bags and hairy chins
shake their heads and reminisce.

I think of those lines by Yeats
and ponder what I might have wished
had I been blessed with my own child.

I might have wished an easy birth,
a calm sleep, a room
innocent of shadows.

I would have wished good friends,
summers of white clouds,
sun like the tang of orange ice on tongues.

Later, I would have wished for her
the first dance and the last
and all the dances in between,

then the comfort of her own space
and the grace to like her own company
until she was ready to answer someone's smile.

I might have wished a happy motherhood,
a table full of friends and family,
a study filled with photos, songs and books.

If there had been time I might have liked
to carry my own child along the aisle
of a tilting train that's running on and on.

CHAPTER 30

Family news

Woodlands
2nd February 1866

Dear Cousin Forristal

This has been yet another year of many changes, some happier than others. For the past year I have been mother to a new born child, the daughter of Joseph and his wife Lizzie, who sadly died giving birth to her.

There had always been the danger of a troublesome birth for Lizzie was already 35 and it was unwise to think of motherhood. I tried to make her rest during the final weeks but she was of a stubborn frame of mind and refused to let me help her. When her time came, it was clear we must call for the doctor but by the time he came it was too late to save her. It was only by God's grace that the little one survived.

We've called her Elizabeth Margaret because her aunt Eliza acts as Godmother. We hope that you will stand for Godfather, although from a great distance. We hope that some day she might have the opportunity to travel home and see those people and places that remain so dear to us. Joseph was distraught in the weeks afterwards but rallied when he remembered his responsibilities. He has been working at an Auctioneer's firm in Berrima for the past month and is doing well.

Meanwhile, you would hardly recognise your old spinster cousin. Elizabeth keeps me busy from dawn to dusk and beyond and there is so much to do each day, there is no time to fret. I believe that Providence brought this little child into my life and I will ensure that she lacks for nothing. In time I shall send you a likeness of her.

As for other news, Mike continues well and expands his flock constantly. As for Thomas, he has for the past year been editor and part proprietor of the "Freeman's Journal", a position he got through the offices of Edward and Dr Quinn, the Bishop of Bathurst. He has a fine time, reporting all the doings of the colony.

In the act of writing these lines, dear cousin, your own letter of the 15th September has come to hand. I am glad to hear that the family is faring so well – it was particularly good to get news of young Margaret and her prospective suitors. I will await with interest further news of all births, marriages and deaths in the parish.

Mike, Bridget and Kate unite with me in a thousand fond remembrances to you, dear old Forristal, Aunt Bessy, Margaret, Ellen, William and the dear boy John.

Yours, Margaret Butler

Darling Point, Sydney
December 1, 1873

My dear Forristal, Uncle Martin and Friends

Forgive me for not writing sooner. I wished to wait until I could announce our great news – Edward has been appointed to the Chief Justiceship of this territory. It is a signal honour, as you shall see. I am sending you the papers that will give a full and proper account of proceedings.

I continue to take care of the motherless child, who is growing fast and is the very image of her father. There is no change since last I wrote.

All is busyness now so I must wait to write a fuller account.

All the Butlers unite with me in wishing you good health,

Margaret

Woodlands
13 February 1874

My very dear William

Your letter and paper with the sad news of your dear Father's and my most beloved friend's death reached me in late January. It was indeed a fine tribute to him in the *New Ross Standard*, much deserved and bringing back many memories of Old Times.

He was for thirty years and more my correspondent ever kind and true. I and my brothers and sisters loved him with a deep affection that neither time nor distance dimmed. I am consoled that the closing of the evening of his long and eventful life had been so peaceful, attended as it was by all the sacraments and offices of the Holy Church.

My dear Aunt Ansty is now my only old relative in the Old Land. I was glad to hear that she and all the other Joyces continue well. We too fare reasonably well here, and prosper, though time takes its toll. But Eliza Meg is a great consolation to me.

I unite with my brothers and sisters to commiserate on your great loss, and to offer you our fondest remembrances.

Your cousin, Margaret Butler

Extract from Fiona Sheehan's journal
15th June 2003

Margaret 24

All over.
I thought
I would know
would feel
the snap
of sinew
All those years
his letters
like
sentences
completed
for me
Old friends
divided
by nothing
more than
the slant
of ink
the smell
of finest stock

Margaret 25

I remember

We stood
on the old bridge
one August night
the air sweet
not a breath
between us.
I barely felt
your hand
on my back
as we watched
the stream
ripple the stones.
All at once
a dart of blue,
a flash of orange
skimming
over water.

A gift
you said,
naming it
though I
already knew
this king
of fishermen.

The first
of many gifts,
Forristal.

CHAPTER 31

Hail and Farewell

I

Good old Flo. It seems
there's an Australian Irish Society
who often invite visiting Irish writers
and Flo has swung for me
an all expenses paid trip
to Sydney to do research
and give the first reading
from the Butler saga.

No title yet, but if
'work in progress'
was good enough for Joyce,
it's good enough for me.

A 22-hour flight first class,
a rental car, a good map
to help me rediscover
where Mags Butlers left her mark.

II

Manchester Airport 18th June 2003

BA257 from Newark was delayed.

I hung around arrivals,
watching the crowds, the ebb and flow
of greetings and farewells,
trying to guess the story behind
each meeting up of parents, lovers, emigrés.

In my bag, an air-ticket newly sent by Flo,
my head buzzing with the trip to Oz,
the sequence that I'd read,
learning their voices,
practising the nuances of
Lizzie and Margaret,
at the same time practising
the speech I'd learned off,
my welcome back to Mike.

Suddenly I remembered how once
when my father was returning home
from some work trip or another
and my mother brought us along
to the airport

I couldn't be contained
when I saw him
through the frosted glass,
raced out of her grasp past
smiling customs men to where
I could hug his knees and cry for Daddy.

He was pleased, though strove to hide it
beneath the facade of disciplinarian
he tried to keep with us.

I don't know how my mother looked,
if she was panic-stricken
when her four-year-old took off
through the crowds,
whether she smiled when she saw
her man come out with her little girl
or was she merely dutiful by then,
stretching her lips, going through
the motions of the waiting wife?

And it scared me that I didn't know
how my face would look
when Mike came out
through that frosted glass.

He was there, striding through
as if there was no-one else
in the arrivals hall,
smile wider than ever.

And I knew how it would go,
this *ave atque vale*
at the meeting point,

there was no home
I could welcome him to.

III

Beaumaris, 20th June 2003

A morning to take flight;
mountains pink-tipped,
dawn sky purple still,

surface scratched by two jets
tearing their orange wakes
in opposite directions.

No wind and low tide,
the Straits a mirror
which geese glide over,

forming their pattern,
slotting into shape
before lift off.

A ragged order,
a V drawn by a five-year-old
on a crumpled page.

They gain height, desultory honks
give them shape, purpose
as they find their route, or follow.

Below, a motley crew.
Herons pause, albeit in slow motion,
a curlew pipes them off.

On shingle, a grey shape;
a cockler crouches as he rifles kelp, searching
as if the earth-bound have the answers.

Postcript

Irish Sea, 21st June 2003

We head into the sun,
turn our face to salutations,
our back to the dark east,

its morning promises.
The sea rocks us asleep,
a gentle port to starboard.

Halfway back, a gull, lost.
Light catches its beak,
perhaps a trick of the perspex.

The waves flatten out as if
there's suddenly space
for all that water

in this place of no coasts,
no harbours,
no moorings called home.

About the Author

Nessa O'Mahony was born and lives in Dublin. Her poetry has appeared in a number of Irish, UK, and North American periodicals, has been translated into several European languages. She won the National Women's Poetry Competition in 1997 and was subsequently shortlisted for the Patrick Kavanagh Prize and Hennessy Literature Awards. Her second poetry collection, *Trapping a Ghost*, was published by bluechrome publishing in 2005 and her third, *The Side Road to Star*, is forthcoming from bluechrome in 2009. She was awarded an Irish Arts Council literature bursary in 2004 and an Artist's Bursary from South Dublin County Council in 2007. She is currently Artist in Residence at the John Hume Institute for Global Irish Studies, University College, Dublin. She is Assistant Editor of UK literary journal *Orbis*.